WHAT COLOR
IS YOUR
EVENT

THE ART OF BRINGING PEOPLE TOGETHER

DIANNE BUDION DEVITT

Dear Liz,

Here's to all you do —

Dianne

Devitt, Dianne Budion
ISBN -978-0-578-04169-8

10 9 8 7 6 5 4 3 2

This book is dedicated with love to my
Mother and Father, Lorraine and
Larry, who taught me that caring
can make anything an art, and that
making people feel special is the
great privilege of life.

di • an • nize *(verb)*

1. to cause sudden, positive, unexpected emotional responses that enhance an ordinary experience through the use of props, tools or production elements.

2. to provoke and encourage play and interaction throughout a meeting/event experience using creative elements and perfect timing.

3. to leverage the power of a well-designed meeting and event to support and enhance an effective print, broadcast, or on-line advertisement and/or a powerful public relations campaign.

4. to combine unique, creative, high-impact design, communications and production enhancements that will make a gathering "come alive" and stimulate the senses of participants.

Writing a book is a lot like planning an event. There's a lot of work up-front that most people never see. When the vision for this book came to me over eight years ago, I had no idea what direction it would ultimately take. How could I get down on paper something that would encompass my whole world?

This book had the special challenge of requiring not only a wealth of words, but also a wealth of creative illustrations. Through writing the words and finding the pictures, I learned, reflected and relived my experiences. I realized, by the end of the project, how very thankful I am to be in this wonderful industry, which allows us to bring people together, both physically and emotionally, by orchestrating and designing live events.

My appreciation and gratitude for their support goes to the many colleagues, family members, and friends who helped me, and especially to my students, who continue to teach me and inspire me with every class. I once read a story about an elderly woman sitting at the window watching her family at a reunion eating, playing, and laughing. When someone asked her why she was sitting alone watching, her reply was "I'm not watching; I'm jumping rope, I'm dancing, I'm celebrating – look." I feel a litttle like that woman when I look at the map and count the many countries and cities where my students live or hail from. I am extremely proud of what we have created together over the years, much of which has spread across the globe. It is wonderful now to celebrate my students with this book.

I am grateful, too, to all the customers and clients, many of whom are dear friends, who have given me the opportunity to make their vision come into fruition in a meeting or event. Thank you all for putting up with me.

A special "thank you" goes to my colleagues and fellow teachers at the New York University Preston Robert Tisch Center for Hospitality, Tourism and Sports Management. Your dedication and support of educating the industry makes me proud to be included as a member of the faculty.

My gratitude is extended to the many industry partners and friends who have supported me over the years, some of whose work is referenced in various points throughout this book; you are the people who developed the business into what it is today and I am proud to have grown with you. I am indebted to Brandon Toropov, whose help and guidance and occasionally fiery debates challenged me to find the words, to assess their meaning and to deliver what I had to say. I am thankful to my creative Art Director, Anthony Parisi, whose talents and abilities helped illustrate the words between these covers and bring them to life. Others to whom I am grateful for their time and invaluable contributions to this project include Celia Gentry Gannon, Mary Lynn Novelli, Jim Alkon, Ayesha Osmany, Pegine Echevarria and Karen Giombetti for her creative research and insight.

To the countless people both in and out of the industry who trusted and inspired me on my journey over the years – I can only say "Thank You." You are forever in my heart.

If you are not willing to change the way you look at meetings and events in today's society, then you can close this book now.

I have been in the meeting and events industry for over 25 years. I have arranged flowers, chairs, and agendas. But as the world has changed, so too have the requirements for those of us in the hospitality business. I like to think that I have adapted to the environment and seized opportunities as they have presented themselves. In effect, I've analyzed emerging new professional identities for people in our industry, which I'd like to share with you and offer for your own consideration.

The concept of planning and the role of a planner is unrecognizable today compared to where it was when I started. The changing economy has altered the corporate landscape in dramatic ways, resulting in fewer meetings and events. Budget cutbacks have led planners to adapt to a series of major changes in priorities and in their own roles.

A lack of understanding about the significance of meetings and events has fostered some unfortunate, and unwarranted negative perceptions about the industry. Thankfully, trade groups and politicians have set out to support the industry and re-educate the public and business sector about the value of meetings and events, and their importance in the corporate equation.

TWO TYPES OF PLANNERS

There are two types of planners. The first type basically inherits an assignment and decides on a series of logical options to make the meeting happen. These planners fill an important function, and their work will always be needed. Every live meeting needs a venue, a room, a layout, a design and appropriate food, beverages, and accessories.

The second type of planner has a very different job. This person makes it his or her responsibility to take an assignment, any meeting, his or her position, and the profession itself to the next level. Such planners are concerned with fulfilling a strategic objective.

Accordingly, they are concerned with a flow and feel – not just a look. They nudge their way into the corporate mindset to participate at the highest level possible, to earn the trust and respect of senior management, and to appeal to the needs, and emotions of attendees. They make it their creative responsibility to deliver an event that inspires and motivates to the point of effectively communicating the intended message and increasing the chances of achieving the intended business result.

This is where I come in.

I wrote this book to help extend the boundaries of a planner's influence and creativity. No doubt, the basics of planning a meeting will always be an important element to the success of any event, but there's a bigger role, one that adopts the philosophy of seeing meeting and event planning as a way of building and supporting a brand, making a corporate statement, and reinforcing that message. Using this philosophy, planners can get the attention of the corner offices, which means they have access to the strongest way to help change and influence behavior.

WHO IS THIS BOOK FOR?

This book is written for experienced planners, many of whom may already be familiar with the types of stories and experiences that appear here. The book also has a special place for the less experienced, or even part-time planners and students who are looking for inspiration as they consider our industry as a career path. The book also has value for those executives and managers who have little to do with meeting and event planning in their day-to-day responsibilities, but see meetings and events as more than just a balance-sheet line item.

In this book, I'll take you through some inspiring and creative stories I've uncovered that show what to do — and what not to. Together, we'll see how "theme" is the central element that starts at a company's front door and carries through the final sendoff. More importantly, we'll see how meeting and event professionals, with the proper tools, talent, and desire can make a difference in the corporate world like never before.

I believe that meetings and events are the blank canvas we can use to connect with each other. So, get your brushes out, and let's start painting!

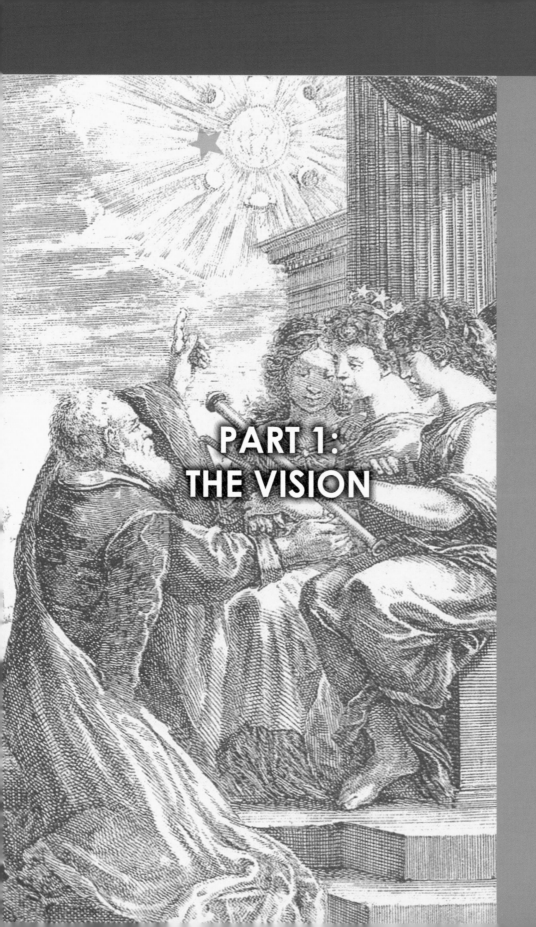

PART 1: THE VISION

It's time to move forward with a robust plan of reinvention both personally and professionally

BUILDING AN EVENT

The experience we create through a meeting or event is as carefully designed and structured as any building. In fact, we can think of the process as architecture. This kind of "building" takes careful planning, just as building a house, office, hotel or museum. It also requires vision, thought, and creativity. It demands a deep understanding of the goals and characteristics of the people living, working, and assembling in the space.

There are strategic, logistic, and creative considerations involved in designing and adapting event spaces. And the most experienced meeting and event planners have evolved from task-oriented staffers to a much more corporate results-focused mentality in response to these challenges. The seasoned planner identifies with words like theme, design, messaging, and flow — all in the spirit of achieving corporate objectives and goals. To execute those objectives and goals, the event professional must master three core concepts I call **Visual Dynamics**, **Kinetic Engineering**, and **Risk Management**.

Visual Dynamics describes everything the guest will see that connects to the pre-event, live event, and post-event experience: the web site, the graphic design, signage, carpet color – basically anything the guest processes with the visual cortex. Each component contributes to the final mental picture of the event. The visual impression will remain in the guest's emotional recall for years.

Kinetic Engineering ties the idea of design to the principle of movement – kinesis. Successful events are all about movement by design. What is the energy flow in the room? How are the traffic patterns in the room? What direction will they take? How will the physical placement of furniture, stage, food, beverages, displays and audiovisual elements affect participants' first and subsequent lasting impressions? Are we creating intimate vignettes that allow for allowing for private conversation?

Risk Management is a critical part of the design process, because what may seem like the best concept for a meeting or event may raise issues that require new thinking. Risk management means understanding what guidelines need to be followed and what rules need to be adhered to. Risk management connects to design because it establishes a carefully orchestrated chain of command, as well as a sequence of events that is vital to the success of the event. These events typically include but are not limited to: obtaining permits and licenses, choosing the right communication tools, understanding copyright laws, negotiating contracts, outlining emergency plans, working with security and police, defining protocol in event of disaster, and so on. First and foremost, risk management means establishing the right face-to-face meetings with the right people leading up to the event, during the event, and following the event.

Are you starting to get the picture about the evolution of the profession as a business discipline?

THE NEW MEMBER OF THE CORPORATE COMMUNICATION TEAM

Perhaps the best way to explain the misunderstandings associated with the meeting and event planning functions within the corporate world is to consider how many different operational areas and/or organizational setups they fall under. Of course, some larger companies have a stand-alone meetings department. This function could also report to corporate management, marketing, public relations, travel, facilities, sales, finance, procurement, or human resources.

Some companies have full-time in-house planners on their payroll; many make meeting and event planning a part-time responsibility of anyone from an administrative assistant to a marketing executive. You can't imagine how many different titles appear on the business cards of people who are involved in meeting and event planning functions; most of them won't even have the words "meeting," "event," or "planner" anywhere on their business card. Many companies rely on outside independent meeting and event planners to either supplement the work of their in-house staffers or handle the role altogether.

It is time to develop a more uniform structure, one that integrates meetings and events within corporate communications. Some firms have already seen the light and begun this process.

These companies recognize that, like advertising and public relations professionals, event professionals are key players directly accountable to the executive team. We manage and coordinate an extended team of specialists who perform various tasks. We are responsible for decrypting non-tangible objectives and goals, and applying learned skills and techniques in support of those objectives.

These three groups of professionals — working in the complimentary fields of **meetings and events, public relations, and advertising** — are delivering and sending messages, generating "impressions" that must relate to each other. It is simply a natural progression that we should be working toward. When I share this principle with senior executives – CEOs, VPs of Marketing, and heads of advertising agencies – they instantly "get it."

Meeting and event professionals have had defined roles for years, but today their responsibilities are undergoing major structural change, both internally and externally. On the horizon is a paradigm shift of titles and roles that will result in internal and external account executives servicing clients and relaying critical information, while others hold responsibility for execution. We have an obligation to continue positioning ourselves as the critical

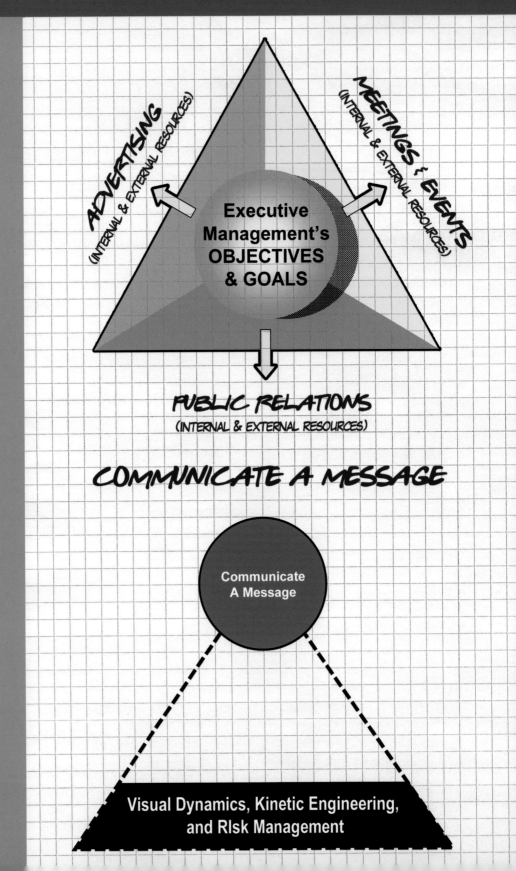

strategic players that we are, and to hasten the day when leading business schools insist that students pursue electives in meeting and event planning as they currently do for courses in public relations and advertising. Until that day comes, we must continue to market ourselves as the professionals we are and educate the customer about the astonishing power of event planning to teach, change, reinforce human behavior, and, most of all, to inspire.

THE POWER OF INSPIRATION

The dictionary defines "inspiration" as "the act of inspiring; the quality or state of being inspired." If we dig a little further, we will find that the underlying idea, "to inspire," means "to fill or affect with a specified feeling or thought; to influence or impel." In other words, inspiration is the act of motivating others by putting them into a peak emotional state — which is what we in meetings and the events industry do for a living. We have no greater responsibility than the responsibility to bring about this "quality or state of being inspired." Our real job is "filling or affecting" people with feelings or thoughts that will "influence or impel" action in a single, consciously chosen direction. As an event planner, you are responsible for helping people move forward together. That's a major responsibility!

So, what does it look like in action?

INSPIRATION IN ACTION

Not long ago, I worked with a CFO at a multinational company; I'll call him Sam. Sam was planning an event that involved senior team members coming in from all around the world to meet collectively for the very first time. At first, Sam and I talked about his goals for the meeting, and it quickly became clear to me that Sam's first instinct was to stay in control, minimize risk, and avoid any detours. Every time I suggested an idea, every time I said, "What do you think we can do with this, Sam?"

Inspiration (literally, "in spirit"):
Motivation from within for outward results

Sam would reply, "Thanks for asking, but I really don't want you to do anything." He was envisioning a "routine" event. Well, I didn't tell Sam, but I was determined to find a way to add value and support his message anyway.

Our discussions uncovered that the big idea for the event — the compass point we would be moving toward — was the theme of **Balance** in executing the company's financial strategy. I thought to myself, "Okay, fine, I'll start small for Sam." I went out and bought some of those little momentum-ball games that you find on the desks of executives. You know the "executive toy" I mean: the little silver ball swings and hits four other little silver balls, which causes one ball to swing out on the other side and then swing back and hit the same balls. I tracked down two of these little desk toys, which are all about the balance of force and momentum.

The day of the event came. I placed the two props on the registration desk, which was technically a neutral physical space and not part of the event space. Before long, every attendee who came up to the desk started playing with the "executive toys." As expected, during the breaks, people were gathered around the reception area, trying to be the next ones to swing the little stainless-steel balls!

Those little desk toys were what I call **Event Enhancers**, and they arose out of my background in Creative Dramatics. In the theatre, you must engage an audience – no ifs, ands, or buts. In meetings and events (and in adult education), you must engage participants – no ifs, ands, or buts. The desk toys were tools I used to spark involvement, and direct people toward Sam's point on the compass. They transformed the physical registration space in a way that inspired participants to connect with, and remember, the larger idea of balance in executing the company's financial strategy.

The desk toys were put out on the morning of day one. By lunchtime, I had privately introduced four new concepts for additional Event Enhancers to Sam – all of them in support of this idea of balance – and, as I expected, he started saying "Yes" to the new ideas. In fact, he started changing his presentations to prepare for the right moment when these new ideas would have the most impact. Together, we built the power of inspiration into that meeting as we went along. Sam observed how Event Enhancers were inspiring people to connect with his message. He liked the results he was getting using these simple toys and props. We turned the meeting around; attendees started to look forward to what the meeting was going to bring to them next.

At another event I worked on, the CEO was on stage during the opening general session. It was a pivotal meeting, bringing in a whole new executive team after a controversial management shift. During that morning meeting, the CEO said, "Now, more than ever, I need a team who knows how to walk and chew gum at the same time!" When I heard that, I realized: That was the big idea! That was the point on the compass we had to direct people toward. I ran out to my assistant and said, "Go out and buy 200 packs of Big Red gum!" (Red was one of the company colors.) She began working on that. At the same time, I went to the business center and ordered 200 small printouts that I could set up on break tables: The printouts read "Building a team that walks and chews gum at the same time!" When the doors opened for the morning break, there were packs of gum and printed cards scattered on all the tables. My client experienced the big idea by means of the Event Enhancers I had created on the spot. He smiled, walked over to me, and said, "How did you do that?"

I did it with Event Enhancers – by using them to create a theatrically participatory environment. (You'll learn more about Event Enhancers on page 77. Also, see samples in the Appendices section of this book.)

Event Enhancers are physical objects, tools or props used to tell the story, to support the message, and to evoke emotional response.

Event Enhancers are to meetings and events what plots and subplots are to theatre and film. They build the story on emotions and engage the participants.

Twenty-first century event professionals provide critical expertise in the "live theatre" of experiential marketing and brand perception. We bring professional standards to the essentially theatrical, deeply interactive work we do in concert with marketing, advertising, and public relations efforts. In fact, our professional practices are now becoming so well defined that people in the advertising and public relations fields are increasingly eager to partner with us in carrying out the organization's strategic vision. Senior decision makers too, realize the powerful advantages that public relations and advertising campaigns can achieve by synchronizing their efforts with a well-executed meeting and event. A decade ago, I realized that, to make this synchronization possible (and seamless), I needed a process. By re-inventing ourselves and our roles, we re-invent others perception of us and affect the entire industry's growth.

THE EVENT DEVELOPMENT CYCLE – IT'S A PROCESS!

I developed the concept of the Event Development Cycle about 10 years ago, while delivering a presentation that described a meeting and event from conception to completion. The purpose is to show the origins and phases of the event, and to demonstrate the compatibility of meetings and events with the more established business communication vehicles of advertising and public relations.

I believe the trend of interaction of advertising, public relations, and meetings and events will continue to reveal the natural affinities and relationships among them. New possibilities will continue to emerge for using these forces of communication as vital, and interconnected business components working together to deliver and reinforce coordinated messages to a wide range of critical constituencies — messages that support brand initiatives, strategic plans and corporate social responsibility initiatives among others. Meeting and event professionals must take part in both strategic and tactical discussions to determine the format and execution of these messages. The Event Development Cycle is designed to support this interconnected relationship of advertising, public relations, meetings and events.

LETS LOOK AT THE MODEL

The **Event Development Cycle** model takes the form of a pyramid that demonstrates the interrelation of vision, strategy, design, execution, and logistics.

The model that resulted has since become a central part of my consulting, training, and speaking work.

Take a look at the diagram. Its purpose is to show the phases of the event, and to demonstrate the compatibility of meetings and events with the more established business communication vehicles of advertising and public relations. These three disciplines provide a company with the capacity to maintain integrated, effective communication about their products and services; to sell, promote, and build acceptance in the marketplace; and to reinforce these messages through the live theatre of meetings and events.

THREE INTERCON- NECTED DISCIPLINES – ONE STRATEGIC MESSAGE!

Advertising disseminates information through television, cinema, radio, print, direct mail, outdoor, transportation media, the internet, social networking, interactive, and other media. It generates positive emotional responses by means of multiple "impressions" of the corporate message, urging a direct, experiential reaction from the reader: buy me, click me, use me, smell me, and so on.

Public Relations has the responsibility of building positive rapport with the public by designing and shaping both mainstream and non-mainstream media coverage. It generates and influences human responses by means of multiple "impressions" of a given message. Strategic public relations campaigns address, and change perspectives on a given issue within the perceptions of a specific audience. The focus is on who covers a story and how.

Meetings and Events bring people together through organized, interactive, live environments that are meant to be experienced as a participatory event. The event must generate emotional responses by means of a succession of "impressions" that create live theatre that engages participants, brings the message to life, gives it deep experiential meaning, and makes it easier to remember.

Over twenty years ago, *Richard Aaron*, industry leader coined the term **"Event Architecture"** to describe the logistics of creating an event. I've used the phrase to recognize conception and design as the core of the planning process with strategy infused with logistics, production, and marketing. More recently, an industry colleague in Europe, *Maarten Vanneste* wrote the book **Meeting Architecture** in support of the movement toward a new structural view and a multi-dimensional understanding of meetings and events.

Logistics and execution are manifestations of vision and a well-designed plan. They support achieving the goals.

LET'S FOLLOW THE CYCLE

 It Starts at the Top.

Companies and senior executive management drive the direction of the meeting or event. The cycle begins with vision, defining "super" objectives and goals, the big picture, and a concise, clear message to communicate. There must be a strategy for tying the event to the corporate direction!

 Business Units.

This message then cascades to individual management and business units. The business units may plan their own parallel meetings and events correlating to the "super" objective of the company, given the responsibilities of their own areas.

 Business Units Reach Out to Internal Meetings and Events Management.

These professionals are comparable in level to the business unit heads.

 Senior Meetings and Events Exec Creates a Coordinated Plan.

This individual has the responsibility for delivering the means by which these objectives and goals turn into a memorable, tangible experience. Eventually, I predict the Meetings and Events departments will comprise of a staff of two to four people, outsourcing all services to specialized agencies. One agency may specialize in

THE EVENT DEVELOPMENT CYCLE

MEETING OR EVENT

COMMUNICATE A MESSAGE

- CREATIVE EXECUTION:
  - T.V.
  - PRINT
  - OUTDOOR
  - MEDIA
  - DIRECT
  - INTERACTIVE
  - RADIO
  - SALES PROMOTION
  - INTEGRATED
  - EVENTS

EXECUTIVE MANAGEMENT

BUSINESS UNITS

MEETING & EVENT MANAGEMENT

INTERNAL ACCOUNT MANAGEMENT
EXTERNAL ACCOUNT MANAGEMENT

VISUAL DYNAMICS, KINETIC ENGINEERING, & RISK MANAGEMENT

ADVERTISING CAMPAIGN

DELIVER COMPONENTS

EXECUTIVE MANAGEMENT

BUSINESS UNITS

STRATEGY AND PLANNING

INTERNAL ACCOUNT MANAGEMENT
ADVERTISING AGENCY

- CREATIVE EXECUTION

PUBLIC RELATIONS CAMPAIGN

DELIVER COMPONENTS

EXECUTIVE MANAGEMENT

BUSINESS UNITS

STRATEGY AND PLANNING

INTERNAL ACCOUNT MANAGEMENT
PUBLIC RELATIONS AGENCY

- CAMPAIGN EXECUTION

Public Relations has the responsibility of building positive rapport with the public by designing and shaping both mainstream and non-mainstream media coverage.

strategy and planning, and the other in creative implementation to support the messaging, much as advertising and public relations firms support corporate objectives now. Some existing communication and production agencies will morph into these roles, perhaps combining the planning and creative, but there will be clearly defined duties for both areas.

 Account Management Takes Over.

One of two things happens next. Either someone with the position of Internal Account Manager will service mutual stakeholders within the department as one of the support roles, or this job will be outsourced to external planners and producers. I believe the planner's role and nomenclature, as we currently know it, will continue to be refined as businesses absorb meetings and events into their core operations as communication vehicles.

 The Event is Built.

Regardless of how it is managed, the event is designed and built, following through on the work of the meetings and events executive and implemented by logistical and production teams fully incorporating the responsibilities associated with Visual Dynamics, Kinetic Engineering, and Risk Management. Dialogue is constant.

7. Symbiosis.

All of these steps will work symbiotically with campaigns in advertising and public relations, based on the specific needs and priorities of the message, and combining all efforts with effective marketing.

 8. Launch.

The meeting or event is launched with all the energy and resources it needs to maximize the return.

 9. Measurement.

Working within appropriate budget constraints and guidelines, the message has to be delivered and measured based on the original objectives and goals. The goal here is to learn how effectively the measure reaches and impacts its audience.

 10. Feedback to Management.

A successful event feeds back results and lessons learned to management; the cycle continues, linking past data and experiences with the next event, and leveraging both expertise and relationships that have been accumulated in earlier efforts.

The organization's management, strategy, planning, creative, logistics, and production functions will be seamlessly integrated with marketing, advertising, public relations, and promotion initiatives.

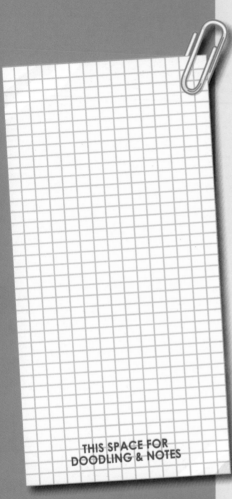

THIS SPACE FOR
DOODLING & NOTES

"WHY ARE WE HAVING THIS MEETING, ANYWAY?"

All too often, the people in charge don't seem to put a clear definition on exactly why they are having a meeting. Without such a goal, it would be impossible to implement all the elements we are talking about ... elements that are crucial to any event's success.

Whenever I work with a client, my first objective is to get direct access to the highest-ranking person I can. My question for that person is a simple one: "Before we move forward with anything, help me understand — why are you doing this?"

The answer to that question may require a good deal of discussion on both sides, because sometimes the real reason for creating an event needs some dialogue to take shape.

To the right, you will find a checklist of possible answers to the question "Why are we doing this?" As professionals in our field, we should be able to check at least one of the boxes on the checklist in answer to that question.

IS THE OBJECTIVE TO:

- ✔ Reward an individual or a team?
- ✔ Recognize a specific achievement?
- ✔ Retain employees, customers, or other stakeholders?
- ✔ Celebrate an important event, milestone, or anniversary?
- ✔ Brand or re-brand a product or service?
- ✔ Launch a new product, service, or initiative?
- ✔ Change attitudes toward the organization?
- ✔ Educate people about an important topic, as part of a larger mission?
- ✔ Inspire people as part of a larger mission?
- ✔ Help people improve their skills in a certain area?
- ✔ Build team cohesion?
- ✔ Honor a deceased luminary?
- ✔ Commemorate a historic milestone?
- ✔ Plan for future direction?
- ✔ Announce future renovations or refurbishments?
- ✔ Prepare for re-structuring or mergers?
- ✔ Reunite the team?
- ✔ Recognize the value of being a team member?
- ✔ Hear a political candidate speak?
- ✔ Recruit new employees, members, or students?

A theme name is the product of the objectives and goals; a theme style is how the story is told.

The task of creating a theme and an appropriate design follows much more smoothly once the event's message and purpose is clear to all the people involved.

ABOUT THEMES

Outsiders might believe the meat of any meeting or event is its content. I say the heart of any event is its character – and that expresses itself through its theme.

A theme is a title or slogan - the catch phrase or big idea that defines your event. No two events are alike. Each event has a unique emotional resonance, which means each event should present a unique theme. The theme determines the personality, characteristics, and universal message.

Identifying the right theme is a serious matter. It means finding the most precise words to accurately bring the meeting's objectives and goals to life. Cities have spent millions of dollars identifying the high-impact tagline or slogan that gives the city an identity. For example, few people can't finish this sentence: "What Happens in Vegas … !"

Choosing the right theme is an art. Just as an artist chooses colors carefully for a masterpiece, our choices about themes must also be made with great care, because they affect the perceptions and impressions of the audience.

HOW TO DEVELOP A KILLER THEME

1. **Begin with a clearly defined objective.** Sound familiar? You can't do anything until you know why you are bringing everyone together. After you clarify and qualify what your client is trying to accomplish, you can begin to build and design the event to support goals and objectives.

2. **Begin with the end in mind.** What impression do you want everyone to leave with after this event? How do you want people to feel? What message needs to be communicated? What actions do you want taken moving forward?

3. **Identify the risk management concerns before any planning begins.** Before the creative process starts, concerns that are obvious risk factors and affect security and safety must be addressed. This applies to both internal and external factors, people, places, and things. This connects with the "Murphy's Law" principle, that if anything can go wrong, it will.

4. **Have a hook.** This is the title, or the series of titles, that connect to your theme and capture its essence. William Shakespeare wrote, "A rose by any other name would smell as sweet." He was wrong! Whether you call the flower a rose or a rutabaga does affect your sensory perception, and every other kind of perception as well. Finding the right hook, the right name, the right tagline, is the point where designing and planning the event really begins. Even if your hook doesn't end up being seen or heard by the public for some reason, you still need to have a hook you can use for your own internal planning. The hook must be concise. It must inspire the look and feel of the event. It must focus everything you do.

5. **Invest enough time in research.** There is no excuse for not doing the right research in the digital age. Look for a two- to-three-year history of similar events – and find out what worked and what didn't work quite as effectively in terms of theme selection.

THIS SPACE FOR
DOODLING & NOTES

6. **Collaborate.** Bring together people with different perspectives, ideas, and talents. Start with a single word or idea, and then brainstorm. Remember, each new idea is like feeding a fire. Each new idea makes possible another new idea. Don't break the chain. Include all the stakeholders, and emphasize possibility as you refine your theme. Note all keywords that relate to internal and personal goals as well as external and big picture goals.

7. **Stimulate the senses.** Think in terms of vision, hearing, sound, taste, and touch. Think of ways your theme will connect on all these sensory levels. Never forget that you are creating a theme that is meant to engage people … and people are sensory beings. Most of our communication takes place non-verbally, and is based on sensory impressions.

8. **Keep it real.** When it comes to choosing the theme that will drive the event, start by thinking big, and then choose what you can actually execute. Be realistic. Can the theme deliver a tangible message with the available resources? Do the creative ideas require labor? Is there enough time? Does the theme have a direct correlation to the reason the event is being produced? How will you design an experience to visualize that theme? What decor options will work the best given the available time, budget, and resources? Will your "show" be simple with minimal props, or will it be "realistic," incorporating all the minute details?

9. **Create the destination.** The theme is all about taking people places. If you can't afford to take them to Maui, you can still build the idea and the setting of Maui into the event. The theme and event is not about a physical place, but a mood, a kind of energy, a state of being. The theme can and should create a sense of place, of community, and of suspension of everyday reality. Consider using the theme to move people to a place they haven't been before, regardless of the physical location.

10. **Make it expandable and adaptable.** The theme you choose should correlate with and support the organization's larger message. It should match up seamlessly with existing initiatives, and be flexible enough to be applied to many different settings.

11. **Sleep on it.** Regardless of how brilliant you think the idea is, give it time and address all of the above before making a final decision. Don't try to force things. Troubleshoot the concept and look at it from every angle.

The right theme is the "Big Idea" that ties together absolutely everything connected to the event. It provides the starting line for all stakeholders and keeps everyone focused on the same vision. The right theme is pervasive. It must be woven into every decision, major and minor.

Perhaps, most of all, the right theme is a major investment. It is not the result of snap decisions; people and organizations spend a great deal of time, effort, attention and money identifying it and refining it.

LET'S PLAY A GAME: A TALE OF TWO EVENTS

Here are two events to consider. Which one has the stronger theme?

EVENT NUMBER ONE: The leadership at Acme Consolidated Products wants to show the members of its sales team how much they are appreciated for the hard work they put in during a tough year. Despite an industry-wide downturn, senior executives want to reward the entire 12-person staff for beating quota, both as individuals and as a team. This is a remarkable achievement, and Acme wants to be sure the team knows how much it is appreciated.

THEME
START

THE EVENT

THIS SPACE FOR
DOODLING & NOTES

Accordingly, Acme's CEO requests a three-day celebration in nearby Atlantic City. Day One has a 1920s theme – because that's what the décor of the dated venue supports; the first evening culminates with a banquet that features the jazz band that happened to play the most gigs at the hotel. Day Two is the same as Day One, only this time the guests of honor are told that the evening will replay the disco music of the 1970s, and they are told to dress accordingly. Day Three features an up-and-coming nightclub comedian whose stock in trade is insulting members of the audience and asking them personal questions in front of their colleagues.

Questions to ponder:

- What message did this three-day event send to the participants?

- What theme united the three days? How will the theme continue after the event concludes?

- What objective was served by the choices of the person designing the gathering?

(In case you were wondering, the correct answers are: "Who knows," "None," and "The participants have no idea, so why should we?")

Compare that story to the following example:

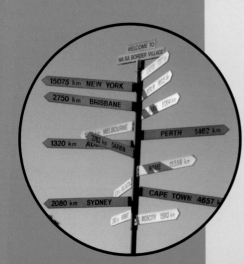

EVENT NUMBER TWO: The CEO of an international technology company gave me the following challenge: "Use the upcoming three-day executive management meeting to make my top executives realize it's time to start thinking differently. I want interaction between the four divisions, and I want the whole company to become more responsive to the marketplace and more interactive with each other. Take all of our left-brained managers and get them thinking inventive, right-brain thoughts, so they approach their business more creatively. I also want them to work together better as a team as a result of attending this event."

Using the CEO's objectives, the Senior VP of Communications and I worked together to come up with the big idea that will bring everyone together around these objectives during this gathering of the company's most senior people. That big idea takes the form of a single word that drives the whole three-day event: "change," inspired by the company's tagline, "Change the Nature of Things."

This event was held for a few years, and each year the theme of the annual meeting added a word to the "change" statement. Year one became "Change the Nature of Things...Together." For year two, the theme was "Change the Nature of Things...Now." Year three continued the theme with "Change the Nature of Things...Faster." These themes reinforced the company's mission statement and also gave direction to the activities of the three days. Everything we did over the three days (and the three years) related to the critical word "change."

To give you just one example of how we used that theme, consider what we did during the "Change the Nature of Things ... Now" year. All the day's events had to do with the idea of supporting rapid, dynamic change, both internally and externally. Each of the events, and

Image: Air Dimensional Design

each of the breaks, was built around a dominant color, and with every progression and event component of the meeting, one dominant color was quickly replaced by another. The breakfast environment was dominated by red, with the pre-function area featuring red linens and organic accents on tables including apples and red flowers. A separate menu was created to complement each color for meals and breaks. Breakfast – red -- featured strawberry yogurt, cranberry waffles, and raspberries for cereal; it was an interactive experience of the theme. The first break changed everything; now the dominant color was white, complete with white-clad chair massage therapists behind folding screens. Lunch was dominated by yellow. The afternoon break was green, so we offered the participants a miniature golf course. Each hole was keyed to an action word from the day's session. The driving message was crystal clear, because it tied into management's objective.

Additionally, each of the four divisions within the company could be presented as a color: **red, yellow, blue and green**. Through the carefully planned interactions and the various event components, you could see a new collaborative spirit emerge around this idea of color. Where once clear, bold colors had divided the organization, new hues began to present themselves. The ever-red engineers began to interact with, and understand the bold blue dynamics of corporate leadership. As a result, a new shade – purple – was created, and a new relationship as well. The same thing happened when the blue corporate leaders interacted with the bright green financial executives: a new understanding came in the form of turquoise. A mosaic of colors began to create a new corporate palette.

This strong, color-driven theme created a dynamic event environment where pre-conceived ideas about specific roles and functions could be stripped away ... and a new corporate vision based on collaboration could emerge in their place.

SWOT ANALYSIS

Only when you have a handle on the theme and its relationship to the event objective, are you ready to start planning your event. The example I just shared with you – "Change the Nature of Things" – provides us a context within which to explore the critical step of the **SWOT** (Strengths, Weaknesses, Opportunities, Threats) analysis that is the central tool for this planning.

In the context of meetings and events, Strengths and Weaknesses describe present-tense happenings; Opportunities and Threats describe events you may encounter in the future.

The SWOT analysis is a four-part business evaluation tool for initial and ongoing examination and self-correction. It should be used for every event – and throughout the event cycle itself, including the planning and design phases.

You must memorize the four major elements of the SWOT analysis and learn to use them routinely in support of your theme. Generally represented as a quadrant, each of the four SWOT elements carries both internal and external data. Internal data relies on the company, organization or event host and its relationships, budget, internal timelines, resources, and technological capabilities. External data includes logistical, environmental and current events.

Let's look more closely at "Change the Nature of Things" and see what went into our international technology company's three-day event. We will use that example to show how to conduct an effective SWOT analysis.

Strengths:
Clear leadership and strong budget.

Weaknesses:
Corporate leadership in transition.

Opportunities:
New leadership offers rare chance to redefine corporate culture.

Threats:
This unproven creative approach may be rejected by technical/engineering minds of the attendees.

Strengths:
Hotel exclusivity and fewer environmental distractions.

Weaknesses:
Negative attendee reaction due to location change.

Opportunities:
To be an exclusive event in a boutique hotel.

Threats:
Potential for inclement weather/difficult travel during February on the East Coast.

Here we have a clear management objective – bring the four divisions of a global company together on both the corporate and creative level. This event (and its supportive budget) were approved by the new CEO, who had recently replaced a more rigid and divisive leader. The new CEO recognized an immediate need to redefine the corporate culture; his goal was to create a seamlessly integrated environment conducive to inter-divisional collaboration. His vision required a large-scale event to introduce this new directive and set the tone for his leadership. From this information, we began to extract the data needed for our SWOT analysis.

After an initial decision to hold the event at a tropical resort, the February meeting was moved to a high-end hotel in an easily-accessible metropolitan city on the East Coast.

Again, each step of the planning process offers information that can be distilled and evaluated by using the SWOT analysis. This business tool should be used for every event, even if you work with the same company year after year. The three years I spent with the technology company required a new SWOT analysis before planning could begin for the next event. Each year, the corporate directive, theme, employee morale, budget and location had to be considered. In short, SWOT provided a solid foundation for the event. Its importance cannot be overestimated.

Here's a complete SWOT example for the first "Change the Nature of Things" event:

Strengths

Clear leadership

Strong budget

Support from corporate executive team

Hotel exclusivity

Hotel layout and design supported privacy and interaction

Few environmental distractions

An award-winning chef was on the hotel staff, and willing to collaborate on creative ideas

Excellent hotel event team

Excellent creative, production and logistical teams

Convenient location for domestic and international travelers

Time and management investment in planning process

Support from executive administration staff

Weaknesses

Corporate leadership in transition

Skeptical expectations amongst upper-management

Hotel has never done this type/scale of event

How to reach attendees on an emotional level without making it personal

Eliminate old corporate behaviors

Limited time factors to execute creative elements

Prevent attendees from feeling "forced" or "manipulated"

Opportunities

To be an exclusive event in a boutique hotel

New leadership offers opportunity to change corporate culture

Hotel chef collaboration with area chefs on event theme

(This collaboration resulted in a subsequent cookbook)

Management support of all creative initiatives

To prove power of meeting to evoke "change"

Threats

Unproven creative approach may be rejected by engineering minds

Due to time of year, potential for inclement weather during event

Travel delays

Perception of the value of creative meeting/event enhancers versus budget spent

Impenetrable negativity due to venue/location change

Lack of hotel staff to assist with quick set-up and breakdown

Potential competition between divisions

THIS SPACE FOR DOODLING & NOTES

The **SWOT** analysis helps to define exactly what design and production elements are being used to execute the theme and message. For example, one of the entertainers during our three day event was an interactive painter. The potential Threat considered in our **SWOT** included setting tables at a safe distance — so as to avoid splattering.

As the SWOT diagram for this event shows, external **Strengths** might include hotel exclusivity and internal **Strengths** include a strong budget and clear objectives from the corporate executive team. The physical layout of the hotel promoted attendee interaction, private meeting capabilities and an environment where attendees could relax and have fun. These too were **Strengths**. Additional **Strengths** for the planner include not having time pressures for set-up or break down, allowing more budget manageability.

Internal **Weaknesses** included the event location change. However, because our job is to transform any potential stumbling blocks into opportunities, this opened up a variety of creative options that were applied to the meeting such as the color 'Green,' and 'Tee Break' which featured miniature putting greens.

Opportunities are creative responses to elements listed under **Strengths** or **Weaknesses**. For instance, you might address the internal **Weakness** of a transitional corporate leadership by positioning executive management in a more informal, accessible role. For example, at our three day event the CEO was challenged to a friendly game of pool by a nationally ranked billiards champion. Because of our sensitivity to the **Weaknesses** identified in our **SWOT**, we were able to break the ice and reinforce team building.

Threats are unforeseen things that could happen during an event. Weather is a classic external threat for outdoor events and activities. Dealing with **Threats** is a matter of assessing and anticipating what could go wrong; this is the Risk Management stage of the planning cycle, and it requires a personal understanding of, and connection to the primary people involved.

Medical considerations, undisclosed dietary concerns, and problems with drugs or alcohol are **Threats** that could disrupt the flow of any event, preventing the planner from proactively finding a solution. Additional potential problems can stem from the use of wires, animals, flames, linens, pools, signage, décor, anything hanging, as well as the possibilities of vandalism and terrorism. Wherever there are people, there are threats and risks to consider.

SWOT is not a one-time exercise. It is a habit that supports and reinforces your theme. Become obsessed with it and use it as a tool from the beginning to the end of the event to keep focus on decisions. The more frequently you examine each element of the **SWOT** analysis, as it relates to the message your theme is intended to deliver, the more successful the event will be.

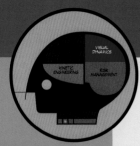

THE IMPORTANCE OF DESIGN

The SWOT exercise you've just seen is, in the final analysis, a design tool. I hope you've concluded by now that design takes on a whole new meaning as we redefine the role of the meeting and event professional. Design is the planning and choosing process applied to the aesthetics and logistics of any undertaking. Design results in a product or action that addresses important questions of form and function. Design solves both aesthetic and logistical challenges by means of good questions that must begin the moment the meeting or event is conceived:

- What statement must we make?

- What is the client's personality?

- What is the most appropriate style based on client's tastes?

- What could this space look like?

- Is the space appropriate to the theme?

- How is it best to direct the flow of people?

- What emotions do we want to evoke instantly?

- What should be accented in this environment, and what should be eliminated?

- What part of my event requires quiet space, and where should that space be located?

- How can we set this space up in such a way as to avoid lines or queues at food and beverage stations – and still leave the space feeling open and accessible?

- What entertainment/speaker/program details must be incorporated?

- Is there a choice about where to put staging?

- Is the space accessible to people with disabilities?

- Where are the exit doors located?

- Should there be a private VIP area, and if so, where should it be located? How can I distinguish it from other spaces?

In meetings and events, design incorporates the essential disciplines of Visual Dynamics, Kinetic Engineering, and Risk Management as components of Event Development. It is the designer's responsibility to interpret and make choices in these three areas.

For instance, the placement of physical objects in any event space has visual, tactile, and emotional implications on the participants' experience. Through the strategic placement of furniture, props, or décor pieces, the designer manipulates and controls the spatial flow, in much the same way a director and set designer plot a stage layout for the theater. Where, when, and how people move is part of telling and experiencing the story.

Design affects everything, and every detail connected to meetings and events should be based on conscious design choices. Great design choices will energize the event and make it easy for people to engage with the message. Poor design choices can undercut the message – and quickly undo all of your good work in other areas.

IT'S A PROCESS – SO LEARN IT NOW!

Everything – absolutely everything – that takes place during a live event must be a deliberate choice that supports the executive team's objective – its vision. To make the right choices in support of that vision, we must recognize the distinct phases of the successful meeting or event. Such an experience is organic – there is no true beginning and end. It is fluid, it is energy that takes on different forms at different times. And it is always the result of choice.

I created the following design based model, which I call **Vision Steps**, to illustrate the kinds of conscious decisions we must make before, during, and after an event.

THE VISION STEPS

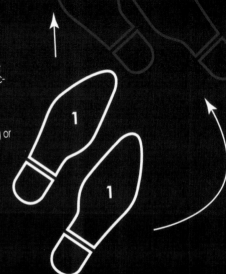

Step 3: Develop
Get feedback from stakeholders.

Determine decor options.

Create a purposeful plan for the entire event.

Create sensory touch points using Event Enhancers.

Step 2: Direct
Conceptualize the theme name.

Choose an appropriate style for the meeting or event.

Start telling a "We" story.

Inspect and finalize the venue choice.

Step 1: Define
Qualify the executive team's objectives.

Identify the audience.

Deduce the "trigger words" or hidden "hot words" that are personal to the REAL objectives and goals - hidden motivation.

Identify what will recur before, during and after the event.

Understand the "big picture" the meeting or event fits into.

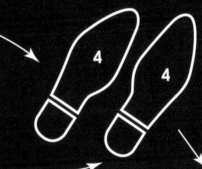

Step 4: Dynamics

Create a clear storyboard that allows stakeholders to visualize the event ahead of time.

Choose forms, colors, textures; identify the visual dynamics.

Establish visual and spatial flow (I call this "kinetic engineering" and it relates the floor plan design).

Get approval and finalize the plan.

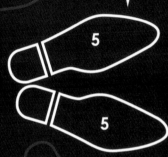

Step 5: Deliver

These are the critical present-tense logistical and decor choices you make immediately before the event.

Set up.

Decorate.

Install.

Display.

Step 6: Deploy

These are the critical present-tense choices you make DURING the live event.

Execute and produce.

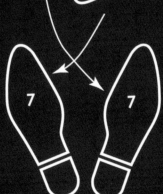

Step 7: Debrief

Go over all your notes and review the experience against the original objectives and goals

Re-connect with stakeholders.

Review.

Discuss.

Dissect, analyze, evaluate.

Set lessons and priorities for future events.

Determine how to extend the message and retain the connection, the impression, the experience until next time

THIS SPACE FOR
DOODLING & NOTES

SOME FINAL THOUGHTS

I believe the real value of a successful gathering lies in implementing the lesson behind Thornton Wilder's classic play, **Our Town**, "We matter to each other." In Our Town, as the characters recall their lives at the end of the play, they don't always remember exactly how the places or faces looked ... but they recall the experiences and the emotional connections. This is the human condition.

An intuitive and experienced meeting and events professional knows that the times that matter most are the times when people come together for a specific purpose: networking or career development, personal growth, or continuing education. These gatherings are all opportunities for emotional connection.

This book shows you how to relay the ancient, emotionally powerful message that matters most of all to each member of your group: You matter, because you are here with us.

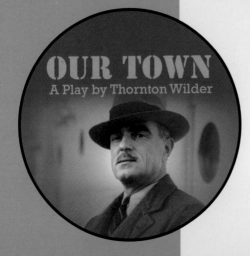

OUR TOWN
A Play by Thornton Wilder

PART 2:
THE BLANK CANVAS

Douglas Rushkoff, a communications expert in the hospitality field, states in his article "The Human Use of Humans: ...Anyone who has ever been to a live event knows that these are the places where the real relationships are forged, ideas are hatched and deals are made."

GO PLAY!

What follows in this book is offered in support of these two simple words: "Go Play!" Centuries before the modern meetings and events industry took shape the Greek philosopher Plato, wrote a book called *The Republic*. In it, he laid special emphasis on the importance of play in developing the full person, the balanced person. Plato's ideas were based on what he had learned from Socrates, the lover of wisdom, who aspired to educate, influence, and engage citizens by "freeing" them through "philosophical play" to live lives of excellence, develop leadership skills, and build and construct a just society for the public good.

In the 1960s, a revolutionary technique called Accelerated Learning was developed, initially for language instruction. Taking a hint from Plato, this school of thought held that people needed more than (boring) classroom environments if they are to learn. Games replaced dry classroom instruction, and proponents of this approach made a number of important breakthroughs about how human beings learn – and why play is so effective in helping them to do so. The traditional lecture-and-reading approach, it turned out, was optimal only to a tiny minority of learners. My personal studies include work in a field called Creative Dramatics. I was fortunate to be in the first graduating class of a remarkable woman named Gertrude Shattner, founder of the Drama Therapy Association.

Ms. Shattner was an accomplished actor whose husband was on the board of the American Psychological Association at the time. I recall her telling us that after he had witnessed the effects of drama games and play, her husband acknowledged and supported the value of play as an innocuous, non-threatening form of personal development that

Typically, internal threats require a clear understanding of the people and personalities involved.

contrasted sharply with the traditional psychological approaches. Creative Dramatics has continued proving the value of imaginative, dramatic play as supported by the accelerated learning methods using games, props, and tools to stress the "multiple intelligences" we all possess.

I insist on the Go Play approach because it is the most effective way of delivering and reinforcing any given message. Play is how adults (and children for that matter) learn best. I believe the reason the Go Play approach works is the same reason virtually all other experiential learning modes ultimately derive from theater and theater games – because they build a sense of instant community, they are emotionally engaging, and they summon an ancient desire to interact and connect with other people. This desire is "hard wired" into our species.

This theatrical connection is the key to making your message – or any message – "stick." Within days, the people who attend your event will forget most or all of the intellectual content, and will remember only the emotions, the heightened awareness, the lessons that derive from strong feeling, and the powerful human connections they experienced. The most enduring and powerful of these memories will be the result of deliberate planning and design of some form of play. How participants connect to the emotions, the experiences, and the people they encounter during the event is your concern. The strategy you use to get people to Go Play is what executes your vision.

There are many studies related to the brain's cerebral cortex and the limbic system that support the necessity of natural play experiences. Attributes related to fear, reward, emotion, social

Image: Air Dimensional Design

behavior, long-term memory, and problem solving all connect to this area of the brain known as the frontal lobe. Like other systems of the body, this area is directly plugged into the endocrine and nervous systems. This fact carries some interesting implications In my view, the employee whose job is unexpectedly downsized experiences something very similar to a temporary lobotomy – and so, for that matter, do all of the colleagues who observe the disrespectful treatment and lack of integrity this person experiences. There is a numbness that sets in; in these situations, people go from shock to anger to lethargy.

The result, at least in the short term, is an internal paralysis that makes meaningful emotional or socially interactive behavior impossible. This is the consequence of interactions that tell people (in essence) that they don't matter. This is the consequence of environments that refuse to permit the possibility of engaged interaction and shared joy.

In 1970, Abraham Maslow, an American psychologist, wrote the landmark text *Motivation and Personality*. In it, he identified the now-famous "Hierarchy of Needs" which is a pyramid shaped structure expressing Maslow's beliefs on what people need to achieve fulfillment and express their own unique potential.

Stop for a moment and think about how much we do within a given meeting and event and how it connects to

THIS SPACE FOR
DOODLING & NOTES

The core function of the meeting or event then, is not to make things look pretty, but to create a safe environment in which to play.

elements of this pyramid: we address needs for food, shelter, a safe and secure environment, a feeling of belonging, and such intangibles as recognition, reward, and self-esteem. It's all there – or at least can be there – in the meeting and event's message. Meetings and events can and should support emotional, intellectual, spiritual, social and personal growth. The meeting or event can only be successful on this level of personal growth, however, if it grants attendees permission to enter the world of the child, the world of play.

A gathering can only succeed when it empowers people to have fun in a safe place where there are no responsibilities, no bills, no deadlines, no distractions, no assignments, and no hidden agendas.

The adult in the business world has an "inner child" who rarely, if ever, has a chance to come out and play. The event is the exception. At most other times in the battles of the daily working world, the shields are up and the assumption is that an attack is imminent. The core function of the meeting or event then, is not to make things look pretty, but to create a safe environment in which to play.

In this safe environment, the participant is given **permission** to allow the expression of thoughts feelings and insights. This environment is where we connect.
Remind yourself throughout this book of the Go Play approach. It helps you to understand attendee behavior, and it allows you to enter a special, magical world of meetings and events where focused play is the rule – not the exception.

A MASLOW INTERPRETATION

SELF-
ACTUALIZATION
VITALITY
CREATIVITY
SELF-SUFFICIENCY
AUTHENTICITY
PLAYFULNESS
MEANINGFULNESS

SELF-ESTEEM

LOVE AND BELONGINGNESS

SAFETY AND SECURITY

PHYSIOLOGICAL NEEDS:
AIR, WATER, FOOD, SHELTER, SEX, SLEEP

If we don't know what the purpose of the event is, or are not willing to measure it, then we will not be able to demonstrate Return on Event.

EDUCATION AND INTERACTION: HELPING PEOPLE DECIDE IT'S OKAY TO PLAY

The moment participants are ready to Go Play, they will begin to engage, interact, offer opinions, alter their behaviors, and even change their values based on the experience designed for them. Education will only occur when there is interaction with the environment and with other people – in other words, when there is the opportunity for play.

This "environmental permission" – which stands in stark contrast to the message environments usually send adults about what they can and should do – typically occurs as the result of a progression of experiences. The best events are designed to fluidly attract the attendee's attention, to guide that attention from one segment of the gathering to another, and to offer continuing evidence that it really is okay to play.

Just as it takes multiple marketing and advertising "touches" to persuade a consumer to purchase a product, it also takes multiple "touches" to persuade a participant to relax and Go Play. I sometimes refer to this decision to play as the critical moment that makes possible a participant's "Aha Moment" – the moment when the message "lands" on the emotional, physical, and intellectual levels.

Without this engagement on the individual level, the message we want to convey will be lost, and the meeting or event will be a failure.

RETURN ON EVENT

Does the kind of play we're discussing unfold without purpose? Of course not. A solid business principle must always drive the Go Play engagement process we have been reviewing: Return on Event.

As event designers, we must have some kind of early, and direct, access to the people who approved the funding for the event if we are to determine the objective, the goals and Go Play activities that will support that objective, and the proper metrics for determining the **Return on Event.**

We must figure out exactly what the event is supposed to accomplish, and how its success or failure will be measured. We must not simply accept an "assignment" for a meeting or event without acknowledging, or even identifying the true strategic purpose of the event. We must not work on auto-pilot. Our job in the early stages is not simply to follow instructions, but to push, poke, and prod senior people – tactfully, of course –into giving us the event's strategic objective ... and perhaps even help them to get clearer on why they're doing what they're doing. We must bring light, a sense of purpose, and a willingness to measure the desired outcomes our gatherings generate: improved brand awareness, improved sales, increased retention of key people, reduced down time, a more robust contact list, or whatever the relevant metric may be. If we don't know what the purpose of the event is, or are not willing to measure it, then we will not be able to demonstrate Return on Event.

To deliver Return on Event, we must rely, not only on strategic input from top people, but also on creative insights from others, both internal and external, who can collaborate with us. There is an art to leading these collaborative discussions – discussions that support the goals of the meeting, create engagement, and ultimately create the environment that generates the individual

THIS SPACE FOR
DOODLING & NOTES

participant's "Aha" response. This discipline, the point at which the aesthetics that support Go Play meet the bottom-line requirements of demonstrating Return on Event – is known as Strategic Event Design.

STRATEGIC EVENT DESIGN

I spent many years trying to identify exactly what differentiates the most effective meetings and events – what sets them apart from the gatherings that fail to "land" their message. The answer, I concluded, was the producer's or planner's mastery of Strategic Event Design.

Strategic Event Design operates both on the "drawing board" and on the front lines; it continually makes creative adjustments by taking the visual competencies of the interior designer and adding to them an essentially theatrical skill: the ability to get participants to respond, and inviting them to Go Play. Film and theatre stylists use props and tableaux to accent their experiences: the positioning of a tree, pillow or piece of furniture affect the look, the feel, and the movement of the actors on the stage, and all of this in turn affects the audience. Simply adding a headpiece or the right hat to a costume changes the entire perspective, and changes how an audience will respond to a character. Theatrical and cinematic communication is virtually impossible without conscious stylistic choices of this kind. Many disciplines convey a message or tell a story: film, theatre, fashion, advertising, and interior design, to name just a few. All of these disciplines manipulate various elements in support of a chosen message: prop stylists, fashion stylists, set stylists, and others change the environment in support of an aesthetic vision. Successful events always have someone on the ground – a Strategic Event Designer – capable of making the same kinds of contributions in support of the strategic objectives of the event.

Strategic Event Designers bring the same theatrical concerns to the world of meetings and events.

Acknowledging this necessity for style in your event means acknowledging the link between vision, conception, strategy, logistics, and production – the link between the elements that are used in the event and the event as it is experienced in real time by the participant. Strategic Event Design connects these seemingly disparate worlds.

Sometimes the Strategic Event Design process unfolds quickly, and the main strokes are laid down on the canvas with breathtaking speed; at other times, the process is slower, with the specifications of the event changing even as the details are worked out. Either way, the strategically inspired planner is standing before a canvas, adding light, color, and life to the event, and bringing the "big picture" together using many elements from her palette: inspiration, experience, and the occasional dash of "twinkle dust" or bolt of lightning. The finished product is, literally, a work of art and one that elicits a powerful (and strategically pre-determined) human response from participants, and a measurable Return on Event.

The Strategic Event Designer enters an empty space with an artist's mind, feeling the energy, envisioning worlds of possibility. He or she begins relating the physical architecture of the space to the visual dynamics and kinetic engineering required to support the event and its theme. The key to opening up those worlds is always the same: asking good questions in support of the event objective.

The Strategic Event Designer is the starter and the finisher who constantly asks: "How can this element of the experience engage people in a way that supports the event's strategic purpose?"

The Strategic Event Designer knows that strategy, design, and décor must be intertwined to keep people engaged and to encourage them to Go Play.

FINISH

SUCCESSFUL EVENT

The Strategic Event Designer is a special kind of artist – one with an eye fixed firmly on the "bottom line" of the Return on Event.

THE ART OF PLANNING AND CHOOSING
In the final analysis, Strategic Event Design is the present-tense planning and choosing process that can be applied to the aesthetics and logistics of any undertaking. Design, by definition results in a product – either tangible or intangible – that addresses important questions of form and function. As we have seen, Strategic Event Design addresses both aesthetic and logistical challenges by means of good questions. Those good questions must begin the moment the meeting or event is conceived, and must continue throughout the process.

- Is the space appropriate to the theme?

- What should be accented in this environment, and what should be eliminated?

- How can this space be set up in such a way as to avoid lines or queues at food and beverage stations – and still leave the space feeling open and accessible?

- Where should the flow of people go?

- What is the format of the meeting or event?

- What do the walls look like?

- What are the walls made from?

- What could be hung on the walls to support the message?

- What is allowed to be hung?

- What do the floors look like?

- What could be placed on the floor to support the message?

- What décor could be placed on a walkway for inter-action?

- What can the columns be used for?

- What is the ceiling design?

- What are the lighting fixtures? Will they affect the stage and room set up?

- What can hang from the ceiling? How?

- Are there windows?

- How can the windows be accented to support the theme?

- What can be done and what can't be done?

- What does the entrance look like now?

- How can the entrance be treated to create initial impact?

- Where are physical doors for kitchen, ingress/egress, loading dock?

- What materials will participants encounter in the room: marble, glass, or fabric?

- How do these materials support (or detract from) the message?

- Where can surprise elements be added for impact?

- What other changes can we make in the environment that will engage participants and help tell the story?

- What part of the event requires private space, and where should that space be located?

- What entertainment/speaker/program details must be incorporated?

- What options are there about where to put staging?

- Is the space accessible to people with disabilities?

- Should there be a VIP area, and if so, where should it be located?

- How can the VIP area be distinguished from other spaces?

- How can all the details be stylized in a way that supports the theme?

The placement of physical objects in any event space has visual, tactile, and emotional implications on the participant's experience of the event.

WHAT IS DESIGN?

Strategic Event Design incorporates all the essential components of the Event Development Process we've discussed so far: Visual Dynamics, Kinetic Engineering and Risk Management. It is the event designer's responsibility to interpret and make choices in each of these three areas. For instance: through the strategic placement of furniture, props, or décor pieces, the strategic event designer manipulates and controls the spatial flow, in much the same way that a director and a set designer plot a stage layout for the theatre. Where, when, and how people move is, after all, an important part of telling and experiencing the event – and of persuading people that it is okay to Go Play.

Design affects everything, and every detail connected to meetings and events should be based on conscious design choices. Great design choices will energize the event and make it easy for people to Go Play and engage with your message. Poor choices can dilute the message and keep people from connecting with the event.

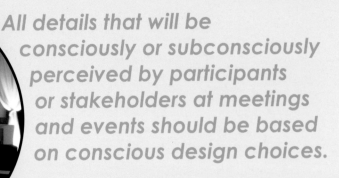

All details that will be consciously or subconsciously perceived by participants or stakeholders at meetings and events should be based on conscious design choices.

Diannize It!

Make room set-up deliberate! The fact that a venue "always does it this way" doesn't mean that that's the way that makes the most sense for a given event. Should tables be set up parallel to the walls in your location (see figure A), or should they be placed at a forty-five degree angle to them (see figure B)

This is a critical design choice affecting much more than seating capacity. The first option blocks the flow of energy and discourages participation and engagement; the second option offers instant visual and spatial interest, and supports energy flow within the room. The choice you make here will have a profound impact on your ability to create an environment that is engaging, secure, and safe.

In the end, design choices always affect the flow of movement, energy, and attention in the room – affecting the ability of your participants to engage with the space you have chosen

and, by extension, the message. Every hotel, venue, and location is different, which means every set of choices about the physicality of a space is different. The challenge is to conceptualize a design plan that engages the audience appropriately and is directly related to the world you are creating and inviting people to enter.

Choices that affect traffic, energy, and attention must always be conscious calculations. Where is the participant's focus going to be? How does that focus support the message? Before finalizing the floor plan, it is important to mentally walk through the event as an attendee to determine what the actual, live experience (as opposed to a drawing) will be. Kinetic Engineering and Risk Management require this kind of walk-through to identify obstacles and spatial flow long before the event begins. This is the only way to create an environment that says Go Play to a participant in real time once the event begins.

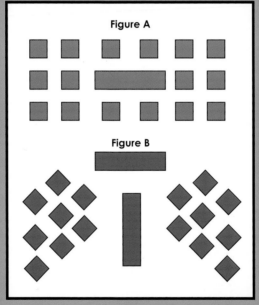

Figure A

Figure B

TRUE-LIFE CASE STUDY: GO PLAY!

Not long ago, I was invited to a distinctly upscale post-Emmy event hosted by a major cable network. The event was a classic example of conscious Go Play event design in service of a clear strategic purpose.

Nominally, the purpose of the event was to honor and celebrate the talent and production teams behind all of the network's nominated shows. However, that was just the stated purpose. In fact, the strategic purpose of the event was to enhance networking opportunities for the people who worked at the cable network, and celebrate with the top industry executives.

To that end, the floor plan and the physical setting of the event were all designed to make it easy for people to gather and mingle, whether in pairs of two or tables of ten. The design encouraged networking and provided a conversation-friendly flow of traffic, focus, and energy. The physical layout of the event, and every detail on the ground, was created to support and encourage social interaction as well as intentional areas where partygoers could "see and be seen."

The theme chosen to support this fete was inspired by interpreting Brazilian art and artists, music and architecture in the spirit of celebration. Notice that this theme had no relationship to any of the network's shows or upcoming

Photo by Gabor Ekecs

features! The night was all about mingling and connecting, being fabulous and over-the-top.

This event successfully sent the Go Play signal, and created positive feelings for the hundreds of VIP and celebrity guests in attendance. It sent the timeless message: *You Are Here Because You Are Special And Matter to Us.* The room's floor plan – with its multi-level design (and distinctive runway-style seating area), and its multiple conversational areas for small groups, demonstrated this.

As a participant, I realized the wisdom of this design approach. The event really wasn't about whether the cable network's shows won or lost the Emmy that night, although it won many, but rather about being in the elite "inner circle" at one of the premiere networking events of the year. I'm happy to say I had a great time at that event and felt like I, too was a network star ... but I'm still waiting for my own Emmy nomination.

THIS SPACE FOR DOODLING & NOTES

PART 3:
CHOOSING THE COLORS

COLOR

DÉCOR

FOOD

COLLATERAL

MUSIC & ENTERTAINMENT

PRODUCTION
(AUDIO VISUAL, LIGHTING , STAGING)

It's not what you use,
but how you use it!

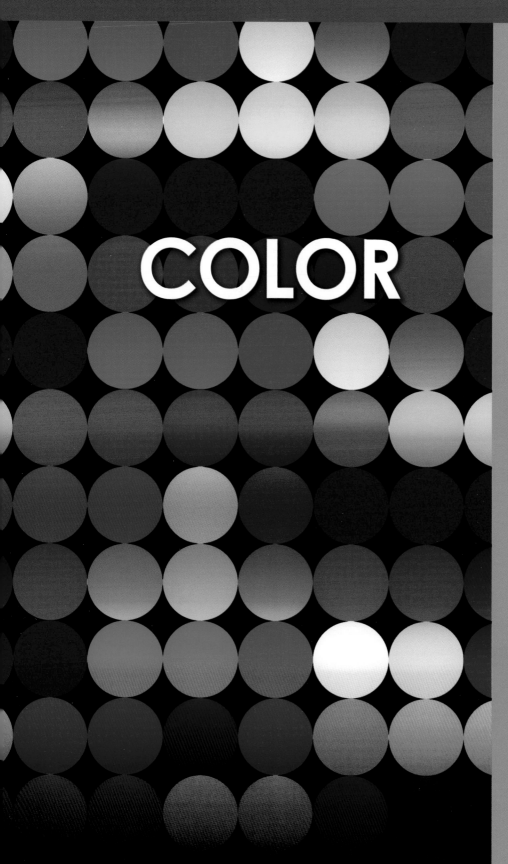

COLOR

"Good design is a Renaissance attitude that combines technology, cognitive science, human need, and beauty – in order to produce something."
Paola Antonelli, Museum of Modern Art

HELLO MY NAME IS

"COLOR IS, IN FACT, ONE OF OUR MOST POTENT GENERATORS OF EMOTION, EVOKING POWERFUL REACTION BY BYPASSING THE 'INTELLIGENT BRAIN' AND HEADING STRAIGHT TO THE 'PRIMITIVE BRAIN' WHERE THOSE STRONG EMOTIONAL REACTIONS ORIGINATE."

Ronald C. Budny

HELLO MY NAME IS

"IT IS PROBABLY THE EXPRESSIVE QUALITIES (PRIMARILY OF COLOR BUT ALSO OF SHAPE) THAT SPONTANEOUSLY AFFECT THE PASSIVELY RECEIVING MIND, WHEREAS THE TECTONIC STRUCTURE OF PATTERN (CHARACTERISTIC OF SHAPE, BUT FOUND ALSO IN COLOR) ENGAGES THE ACTIVELY ORGANIZING MIND."

Rudolf Arnheim

HELLO MY NAME IS

"COLOR IS CRUCIAL...BUT IT IS VERY HARD TO TALK ABOUT. THERE IS ALMOST NOTHING YOU CAN SAY THAT HOLDS UP AS A GENERALIZATION, BECAUSE IT DEPENDS ON TOO MANY FACTORS: SIZE, MODULATION, THE REST OF THE FIELD, A CERTAIN CONSISTENCY THAT COLOR HAS WITH FORMS, AND THE STATEMENT YOU'RE TRYING TO MAKE."

Roy Lichtenstein

HELLO MY NAME IS

"I FOUND I COULD SAY THINGS WITH COLOR AND SHAPES THAT I COULDN'T SAY ANY OTHER WAY — THINGS I HAD NO WORDS FOR."

Georgia O'Keeffe

"COLOR IS SENSIBILITY IN MATERIAL FORM, MATTER IN ITS PRIMORDIAL STATE."

Yves Klein

"THE KALEIDOSCOPE CAN BEST BE UNDERSTOOD AS A METAPHOR FOR A NEW WORLD PERSPECTIVE... WHERE THERE WAS DIVISION, DIFFERENCE, AND APPARENT CHAOS, THERE EMERGES INTEGRATION, SIMILARITY, AND AN ORGANIC UNFOLDING... THE WORLD IS YOUR KALEIDOSCOPE, AND THE VARYING COMBINATIONS OF COLORS WHICH IT PRESENTS TO YOU AT EVERY SUCCEEDING (AND UNIQUE) MOMENT ARE THE EXQUISITESLY ADJUSTED IMAGES OF YOUR EVER MOVING THOUGHTS."

James Allen

The English language is full of catch-phrases that link color with powerful experiences and emotions: green with envy, red with rage, yellow for cowardice, white for purity, blue for "the blues," and so on. The more research you do into the vast and complex question of how human beings perceive color, the more respect you have for these connections.

They are far more than clichés; they are culturally specific signposts testifying to the immense psychological importance of color in the human experience.

The conclusion, over and over again, has been that there is energy in color that affects our well-being, safety, moods, behavior.

How important is color? Renaissance master painters spent months or even years looking for, and making their very own color pigments, in some cases searching the far corners of the globe to create the perfect shade. What propelled that quest? Some of these ancient masters secured the services of "color men" who would provide them with the perfect pigments, prepare their canvases, and make their brushes. Others, like Leonardo da Vinci, preferred to mix their own colors, treating the elements that made up each pigment as though they were precious jewels (which they sometimes were) and mashing, grinding, burning, and crushing natural materials together for just the right effect.

Color was each artist's secret; the way varnish reacted with each carefully ground color on the canvas became part of the artist's distinct style. Would they have simply used each other's pigments and palettes? Of course not! Each hue, pigment, and shade of color was the artist's distinct trademark, just as their aesthetics reflected their own individual styles. They would have regarded using another painter's colors as something close to a breach of personal ethics. *Meeting and event designers, stylists, planners, and producers must be ready to use color to make a unique personal statement, too.*

Countless books, articles, theses, and research studies exist on the question of how color affects human perceptions, emotions, and behavior, and this book is not meant to offer the final word on that topic.

I do want to confirm for you, though, that certain basic color principles have tested in multiple settings. The conclusion, over and over again, has been that **there is energy in color that affects our well-being, safety, moods, behavior.** When color engineers began to analyze the use of color in industrial settings and in public places like schools, hospitals, office buildings, and homes, they focused on the physiological and psychological reactions and benefits these basic color principles supported. The prevailing wisdom now is that the many powerful and impossible-to-ignore responses of human beings to specific colors are due to the inherent energy in color. The power of this energy can be transformative.

Linda Clark, in The Ancient Art of Color Therapy, states that:
"Color, in the form of light, is part of the electro-magnetic spectrum. Light is one of its many octaves; others are cosmic rays, gamma rays, X-rays, ultraviolet rays, infrared rays, radio, television rays – including light – all possessing energy."

Studies have shown, for instance, that a person lifting a dark-colored box or piece of luggage will actually experience that object as being heavier than a light-colored one. (This is apparently the physical equivalent of an optical illusion.) Some pioneering work in the field of color research by Dr. Max Luscher in Basel, Switzerland in the 1940s, broadly known as the Luscher Color Diagnostik, established another important point about color. Dr. Luscher concluded that the "sensory perception of color is objective and universally shared by all, but that color preferences are subjective, which is a distinction allowing for ... individual testing." He meant that most of us see the same or similar colors, but our bodies can interpret those colors very differently, based on the correlations we make mentally, emotionally, and physically through association and memory.

Early and influential work was done in the late 1800s by Dr. Edwin D. Babbitt in *The Principles of Light and Color*. Dr. Babbitt's work served as the forerunner to modern research on muscular, mental and nervous system connections to color. His research showed that when water is stored in a red glass pitcher and left to stand in the sun for an hour, the colored light affected the water,

Diannize It!

Consider using linens within the same color, but with varying hues and textures, when designing a large event.

somehow making it more active – and creating a more stimulating cup of coffee. Alternatively, if water is placed in a blue glass pitcher, the soothing effects of the blue-infused water appeared to affect the potency of chamomile tea – in effect, making it more calming.

I approach the study of color much as I would approach the task of learning another language – a complex language with universal impact. I predict that medical science will soon place much more emphasis on this language, through further research and results about color feedback's effect on the body. If today's discoveries suggesting that we can "speak" to the human body more effectively continue to accumulate, and I believe they will, the implications for the meeting and event planner will be vast.

Not long ago, I had an "aura" photo taken; it reflected the emotional and physical state of my body in colors associated with the seven chakras or energy points of the body.

Imagine a video that could be taken during a meeting or event that would reflect, without dilution, what attendees were actually feeling and how they were reacting at any given moment – translated through color. This kind of activity would take the term "transparency" to another level!

Whether we recognize it or not, the event is using color to send powerful emotional signals to participants – minute by minute and second by second. Color

Image: Cloth Connection, Inc.

choices are too important to be left to chance or whim – but all too often, that is exactly how these design choices are made.

The most talented and effective designers know that colors can have a powerful effect on emotions ... and on budgets.

For instance, the simple principle of using variations of one single color will allow you to leave an enduring impact on each participant. The varying-shades-of-a-single-color approach is simplicity itself – and it's far more powerful than a variety of colors chosen at random, or mindlessly repeating the same color. In fact, this is one of the most cost-effective event design "tricks" of all, one that experienced meetings and events professionals use often when presented with a limited budget.

Here's another color principle you can use to your advantage: Fashion designers, among others, know that using bright colors that "pop" and cause a powerful reaction may distract the observer from the fact that the actual design is relatively simple and inexpensive. Sometimes that "bold fashion statement" is also a "cost-effective fashion statement" – although that's not how the consumer sees it. Take a modest garment, choose colors aggressively, and you can get by with less expense on labor and materials. Exactly the same principle holds true for the meeting and events designer. If the budget is tight, you can use a strong, impossible-to-miss color choice to distract people from the details you can't spend money on. In most cases, no one will know the difference.

In business, the science of choosing the right color for a brand often determines a company's survival. Because each color

Color Research by the Numbers

80
(percent by which color can increase brand recognition, according to a University of Loyola, Maryland study)

23 million
(new sales, in dollars, attributable to Heinz's decision to release a variety of green ketchup – the largest annual sales increase in the company's history, according to ColorMatters.com)

42
(percentage by which phone book ads in color exceed black and white ads in motivating people to actually read the ad; White, Jan, Color for Impact, Strathmoor Press, April, 1997)

Less than .67
(number of seconds the typical black and white image sustains interest)

2 or more
(number of seconds the typical color image sustains interest)

73
(percentage increase in comprehension among meeting participants attributable to color choices. Source: Johnson, Virginia, "The Power of Color", Successful Meetings, June 1992

has a distinct emotional association for the observer, color choices that apply to products and brands play a huge role in determining the reactions of consumers and other stakeholders to the product – and even to the identity of the company.

Branding experts know, and respect, the importance of basic color theory; they focus closely on how to use information about color in a way that supports their objectives. Shouldn't meeting and event planners do the same – and avoid missing a major business opportunity?

In Philadelphia, there was a wonderful event called the "Beaux Arts Ball" hosted by the American Institute of Architects. I remember looking forward, each year, to receiving the invitation for this annual event. Why? Because whatever color was used for the invitation also told me about that whole year's color theme. This was important, because in order to attend, you were required to dress in colors that matched the year's color choices. So in this case, it wasn't just the décor and collateral that focused on the color themes the designer had selected ... it was the guests as well. Here we have yet another color-related secret of meeting and event designers: **Asking guests to wear a specific color.**

During that event, the color choices came to life vividly, helping to make the event fluid rather than static – a dynamic, self-propelled organism. This is an extremely simple, yet extremely compelling way to use color to turn your event into what it really should be: a work of art.

Think of color not just as a personal preference but as a communication tool; don't make color choices impulsively – make them strategically. Show different color combinations to people and get their reactions. Ask:

- What are the corporate or personal colors of the host?

- What are the colors of the competition so as to avoid?

- Which combination best supports the theme and message?

- Which color combination conflicts with that message?

- With the venue?

- With the destination?

- With the season?

- What combinations of colors evoke the emotions you want participants to feel?

Image: PBG Productions

"All people, regardless of culture, share a universal range of emotions, such as happiness, sadness, excitement, anxiety, desire, passion and so forth. The ability to tap into these emotions using correct color choices can increase the effectiveness of a presentation."
– Microsoft Corporation

It's hard to overstate the importance of color trends, forecasts and predictions in our society. Often, these forecasts start in the world of fashion and eventually make their way into interior design, restaurants, hotels, and yes, meetings and events. That means that perceptions of, and emotional associations with colors can, and do shift from year to year.

One of the prominent color forecast sources is www.design-options.com, owned by Fran and Arnold Sude, experts in color trends for fashion and interior design that effect event color trends.

CULTURE-SPECIFIC COLOR ASSOCIATIONS

Failing to understand the intonations and meaning of color in different cultures means leaving yourself open to huge and perhaps unforgivable mistakes – such as, for instance, using a color for celebration that represents death or insult within the society where your event is being held. Individual color responses can come from cultural mores; reaction to color is based in part on those powerful learned responses.

Whenever we are working in a culture that is unfamiliar, we must do our research and ask local experts to share their knowledge about the best color choices. What works in Indiana may not work in India, and

"Everybody needs beauty as well as bread, places to play in and pray in, where Nature may heal and cheer and give strength to body and soul alike."

-- John Muir

The art of communication.

what works in India may not work in Indonesia. In other words, there are always strong cultural factors to take into account ... and at the same time, each participant may respond in a unique and independent way to the colors we choose for the event. This means that extensive discussion and testing of color choices is always a good idea. The more important the event, the more carefully the color choices must be vetted.

The guidelines that follow are based on culturally dominant color references in the United States.

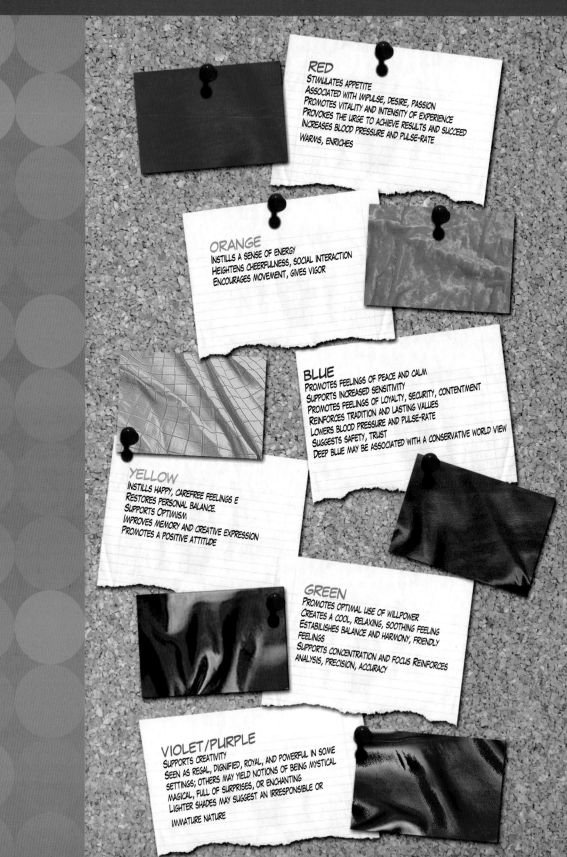

RED
Stimulates appetite
Associated with impulse, desire, passion
Promotes vitality and intensity of experience
Provokes the urge to achieve results and succeed
Increases blood pressure and pulse-rate
Warms, enriches

ORANGE
Instills a sense of energy
Heightens cheerfulness, social interaction
Encourages movement, gives vigor

BLUE
Promotes feelings of peace and calm
Supports increased sensitivity
Promotes feelings of loyalty, security, contentment
Reinforces tradition and lasting values
Lowers blood pressure and pulse-rate
Suggests safety, trust
Deep blue may be associated with a conservative world view

YELLOW
Instills happy, carefree feelings e
Restores personal balance.
Supports Optimism
Improves memory and creative expression
Promotes a positive attitude

GREEN
Promotes optimal use of willpower
Creates a cool, relaxing, soothing feeling
Establishes balance and harmony, friendly feelings
Supports concentration and focus Reinforces analysis, precision, accuracy

VIOLET/PURPLE
Supports creativity
Seen as regal, dignified, royal, and powerful in some settings; others may yield notions of being mystical magical, full of surprises, or enchanting
Lighter shades may suggest an irresponsible or immature nature

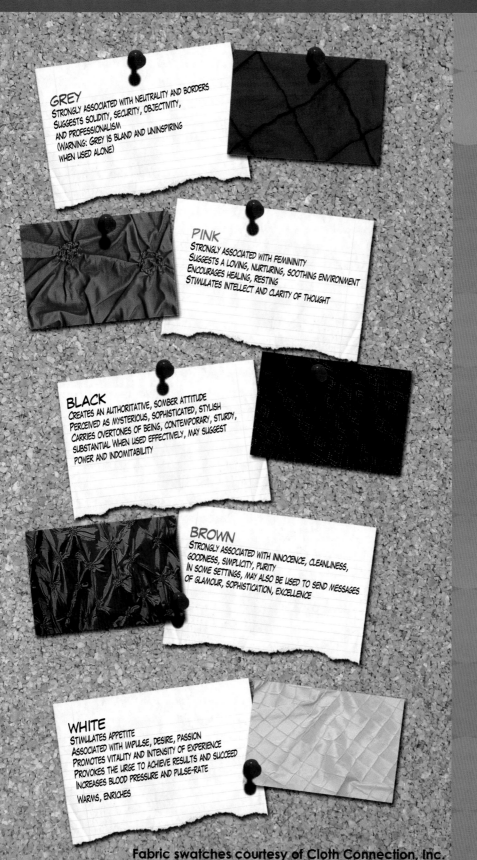

GREY
Strongly associated with neutrality and borders
Suggests solidity, security, objectivity,
and professionalism
(Warning: Grey is bland and uninspiring
when used alone)

PINK
Strongly associated with femininity
Suggests a loving, nurturing, soothing environment
Encourages healing, resting
Stimulates intellect and clarity of thought

BLACK
Creates an authoritative, somber attitude
Perceived as mysterious, sophisticated, stylish
Carries overtones of being, contemporary, sturdy,
substantial When used effectively, may suggest
power and indomitability

BROWN
Strongly associated with innocence, cleanliness,
goodness, simplicity, purity
In some settings, may also be used to send messages
of glamour, sophistication, excellence

WHITE
Stimulates appetite
Associated with impulse, desire, passion
Promotes vitality and intensity of experience
Provokes the urge to achieve results and succeed
Increases blood pressure and pulse-rate
Warms, enriches

Fabric swatches courtesy of Cloth Connection, Inc.

A VINTAGE COLOR GAME YOU CAN USE

Adapted from Ethel Owen's *A BOOK OF ORIGINAL PARTIES*,
Abingdon Press, 1925

Questions

1. What color is valuable and can be worn about the neck?

2. What color do you feel when in state of depression?

3. What color can be found off the shores of Bermuda?

4. What color is the sky on a stormy day?

5. What color is found in the fire?

6. What color are the leaves in spring?

7. What color is very fragrant?

8. What color is phosphorus on the water?

9. What color is often carved and valuable?

10. What color is sour in fruit and pretty in color?

11. What color is well known as a flower?

12. What color is a fruit?

13. What color denotes purity?

14. What color is also money?

15. What color makes you think of "serious"?

16. What color is also a girl's name?

17. What color includes every color but black?

18. What color do you get in summer if you stay in the sun too long?

19. What color does old paper become?

20. What color is also a jewel?

21. What color is both an herb and a body decoration?

ADD YOUR OWN!

The placement of physical objects in any event space has visual, tactile, and emotional implications on the participant's experience of the event.

ree from c... , esp.

dé•cor *also* de•cor (de'kor') *noun*.

1.Style or mode of decoration, as of a room, building, or the like: modern office décor; a bedroom having a Spanish décor.

2. Decoration in general; ornamentation: beads, baubles, and other décor.

3. Theater. Scenic decoration; scenery.

...(dek'e-rat') vt. -rat•ed, -rates. [Lat. de-corate, decorat- <decus,

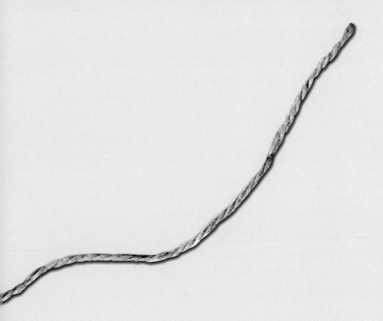

In design, it's always a good idea to look at what you have around you for inspiration. In college, I designed 28 costumes on a $300 budget, using everything from egg cartons to shoe boxes.

The linens we choose are part of our event's décor, so is the glassware we use, and so are the badges we ask people to put on at the registration desk. So is the tent where the event takes place. These are the "tactile" visuals in the Visual Dynamics equation.

Each of these decor elements – and countless others – must embody and illustrate the theme during the live event, and within each décor choice lies a seemingly limitless number of variations. All the décor elements are part of the visual dynamics used in events; they must incorporate choices involving line, balance, form, personal taste, venue, architectural details, shapes, color, pattern, textures, and even interactive elements. And every choice must address the critical question: How, exactly, will this engage the participant?

SOME OF THE BEST IDEAS COME FROM FOUND OBJECTS!

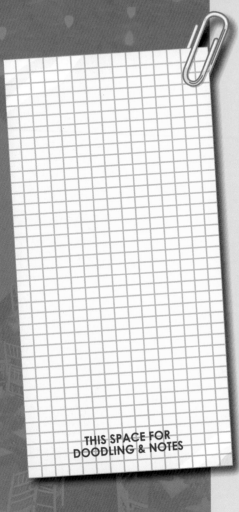

THIS SPACE FOR
DOODLING & NOTES

Realism is natural; symbolism is imaginative.

That question inevitably connects to other questions. What will the emotional reaction to a décor choice be? What will the kinetic impact be? How will this décor choice affect the energy in the room, the attention in the room, the movement of the people in the room? How will all of these choices reinforce the larger message?

Décor is among the first parts of the physical event that the participant experiences. It's what allows us to create the picture, set the scene, and evoke a specific emotion that we feel is appropriate to the experience. Décor allows us to begin telling the story the participant encounters at the event.

In theatrical design, there are two style categories related to décor: realism and symbolism. Realism refers to the goal of recreating an environment that very closely resembles an actual setting, with great attention to detail and nearly exact reproductions of key elements. Symbolism on the other hand, is the discipline that focuses on the imagination first, and physical objects second; the actors might demonstrate through gestures and movements where a wall is supposed to be, or when a cube is supposed to become a stepping stone, a sofa, or a car. Realism is natural; symbolism is imaginative.

The event designer works with a similar, but more complex set of parameters. Meetings and events are not staged with actors who rehearse movements; nor do they follow the rules of interior design and display where the focus is on static visual impressions. Rather, the event designer's

Kinetic Engineering and use of décor must anticipate and guide the physical movements of groups of people. The designer must employ durable design elements that can stand up to the energy of crowds; and must combine elements of both realism and symbolism from the world of the theatre. We need realism to keep the event anchored to a specific theme, and symbolism to liberate the imagination and awaken a sense of play and engagement

Décor must be used strategically and consistently as a multi-sensory tool. Whenever we make choices with décor, we are, ultimately, making choices, not about physical objects, but about the sensory experiences we want our participants to have. That means we are making conscious choices about which senses we want to stimulate, and how that experience will set up the next piece of sensory stimulation we are planning.

Event stylists have to ask: How do all these elements work together? How will the décor choices affect the energy in the room? How will the décor choices support the event theme, the "big idea"? The results of these choices are the Visual Dynamics of the event.

Senses and Sensibility

Good event design must use décor to draw out the senses and capture the attention of participants purposefully, and take them to a specific place. Décor is not a combination of unrelated details, but rather a single coordinated campaign that tells the story via sight, touch, smell, taste, and hearing. Décor includes objects and interior treatment from florals to fabrics, and from furniture to fragrance.

Décor Invites Engagement

Remember that it takes six to eight sensory impressions to "land" a message with a participant. When people arrive at the location, walk into a foyer, step up a flight of stairs, go into an elevator, enter the pre-function area, walk into the room, partake in the reception, or sit down at a table, we must ask: what do we want them to notice first?

A failure to make choices represents a failure of deliberate décor strategy. The ideal is for the participant to encounter, and keep encountering objects and experiences that inspire curiosity, a continuous chain of sensory experiences that feel both brand new and somehow related to one another.

The experience we want to deliver for our participants is not unlike the experience Alice had when she made her way into Wonderland. She kept encountering surprises, **BIG** and small ... objects that kept delivering unique experiences. We have to make sure every décor choice delivers the magic for our participants.

Does the décor speak the message to convey? Does it convey the feeling we want people to experience? Does it create an environment people can submerge themselves in?

If our choices don't support the objectives in a sensory way, we are wasting time, money, and opportunities.

Image: Pink Inc.

Diannize It!

Event Enhancers (see the table on page 184) are a big part of décor. These are not mere "add-ons," but are critical tools that allow us to fulfill our core responsibility to deliver and reinforce a specific message during a meeting or event ... by opening up the minds and imaginations of participants. Event Enhancers give people permission to "play".

Décor, and specifically props, are the key to fulfilling this responsibility. In any given setting, it is one or more of these carefully chosen objects that will serve the special function of making possible **the willing suspension of disbelief among participants.**

Participants are looking for an excuse to participate, to engage, to pretend, to transform, to interact, and to play. We can unlock this desire to interact simply by giving and handing the participant the right tool. It could be a feather, a ticket, a mask, a glow-stick, a funny hat, or even something as simple as a marker for writing on a graffiti wall – but it has to be something to hold.

The idea is not to hand the participant any object, but to hand someone a prop or tool that both engages the imagination and ties into our theme.

Look more closely at the example of the marker used for writing on a graffiti wall: If the event in question is a new product launch tied into the theme of "Passion Sells," and red is the dominant color of the product we are trying to inspire the sales team to get out and sell passionately, then the color of the marker we hand people (and indeed the color that should drive the whole event) becomes obvious: Red.

Or, consider the example of a gala or celebration. Placing a variety of ornate New Orleans-style masks on sticks, and adhering them to the back of chairs, possibly using chair ties, can serve multiple purposes. First, guests have the visual experience of seeing the mask positioned on top of the chair, which gives the illusion of heads. Second, the variety of the masks can make a statement: Perhaps

> *Event Enhancers give people permission to "play".*

you can use them to establish a male/female seating order. Last, but certainly not least, the masks should make a statement about the theme of the event. All of these factors will come into play as guests interact with the environment.

Bestowing the right prop at the right moment in the right place gives people permission to play!

This permission is a "threshold moment." It has a powerful effect on each and every participant's willingness to "drop the shields" and enter a safe place: the environment you have created. Event Enhancers, when chosen carefully, timed strategically, and used effectively, are the glue that holds any event together. They seem simple and spontaneous to participants, but they are actually the result of careful planning and hours of thought and care on the part of event designers. Employ them deliberately; use them to make that all-important "threshold moment" possible, and then to reinforce the theme throughout the event. Use them as threads to tie the message together and keep guests involved.

"It is that willing suspension of disbelief for the moment which constitutes poetic faith."
— Samuel Taylor Coleridge

Dianne's 5¢ rule:

ENGAGE the SENSES!

> *"The first and greatest of life's necessities is food, which is the condition of life and existence." – Plato's Republic, Book Two*

Sylvia Center is a non profit organization that focuses on children's nutrition, farm education, and wellness. As home-cooked meals disappear from dinner tables, America's children face a health crisis. Juvenile obesity is epidemic; and type 2 diabetes, previously unheard of in children, is at a record high. Our programs address this crisis by encouraging children's cooking with wholesome recipes that children can take home and make with their families.

Founder, Liz Neumark,
Great Performances Catering
www.sylviacenter.org

FOOD & BEVERAGE

Diannizing
FOOD

Back in the 60's, there was a saying: "You are what you eat." Indeed we are. Food has an extraordinary effect on human attention, as anyone who has attended a big dinner or visited a farmer's market can attest.

A well-organized display of food can produce dramatic emotional and physiological changes, and even make us feel as though we can "taste" foods at a distance. Think about what happens within our own home. Regardless of how big or small a gathering is, doesn't the company tend to hover around the kitchen? What is it that attracts our families and friends to that part of the house? It's our innate feeling of sharing, gathering together, and nurturing ourselves with food.

Not fueling our bodies properly is akin to not putting fuel in an automobile.

Daily meeting agendas and schedules are typically designed around three meals, with breaks timed to relieve and revive. Yet how many planners take advantage of the opportunity to make a statement with food that supports the strategic message? We are not nutritionists, but we are planners, and we do harness people's energy and attention during meetings and events. *Food is a secret weapon* we can use to achieve both aims.

Just as color affects us, food also affects our ability to focus, become energized, and engage with the message. That means event planners have a responsibility to understand the effects of food types and build balance into their menu choices.

For example, if we're planning a lunch with a full day of interactive sessions following, we may want to focus on the energy that proteins give us instead of serving comforting carbohydrates like pastas, potatoes, and crunchy bread. Those carbs will make people lethargic and affect their focus. We must choose wisely, so as not to sabotage the afternoon's activities.

Not feeding our bodies properly is akin to not putting fuel in an automobile. Be budget conscious, be creative, and be aware of the new level of interest in healthy eating as well as international diets. Help attendees maintain their sustainable energy and attention span, and avoid the peaks and valleys attributed to imbalanced diets.

In 1992, the Institute for Integrative Nutrition was founded in New York City. In the years since, it has become the world's leading nutritional school, teaching the importance of food as medicine and de-mystifying the connection between wellness and nourishment.

Image: Canard Catering

I would like to see a special course designed for those responsible for designing and planning meals for groups – and for the resulting social dynamics.

Use food and beverages as the focus, as décor. Use food and beverages to "edutain" as well as satiate those with discerning palettes. During breakfast, you might have information about the history of the various coffees or teas being served at place settings. These cards can also act as icebreakers; they give people something to talk about. If the location of your event has seasonal products, incorporate them. To add visual interest, consider using raw vegetables as accents and centerpieces.

Get Creative with the Chef!

The most memorable meal I ever had the pleasure of planning was for a Board of Directors meeting that took place in the lovely Berkshire region of Massachusetts. During my initial meeting with the Chef, I asked him what his dream meal would be. That one question resulted in a seven-course chocolate tasting menu, each course paired with appropriate wines. The courses were served accompanied by a ramekin of whatever type of chocolate was used in preparation. Guests were instructed to taste the course accompanied by a chip of chocolate used in the ingredients, and then savor drinking the wine. The memory of this experience still lingers in my mind.

The beautiful (and practical) part is that the meal supported the theme of the gathering: Think Differently. The members of the board had major challenges to address; the innovative menu laid the foundation for some remarkable creative thinking that weekend.

Consult with truly talented chefs; involve them in menu design. Challenge them.

Image:
Canard Catering

Ask them what their dream meal would be. Then look for a way to tie that dream meal to your theme. Chefs are especially likely to be interested if the theme you've chosen is regional or international, or if it involves a specialized type of food. Encourage the chef to think big, and to have some fun with presentation. In any meeting or event, you are looking to create an impression that people will talk about on their way out the door. Once you start collaborating with chefs and other foodies, you will realize that food is one of the most powerful media at your disposal when it comes to delivering that unforgettable impression. People are still talking about that extraordinary seven-course chocolate meal. (Recently, one client shared his own secret with me: challenging a chef to create a meal around a specially chosen bottle of wine.)

Challenge Yourself

Ask yourself: How will my food choices affect the engagement and energy level of the participants? How can food be a more prominent feature of what we're doing here? How can food and food service affect, say, an awards dinner and the production elements that accompany it? What can I do differently with food that hasn't been done before – and also supports the objectives and goals of this event?

Food is a vital creative tool for the planner. The amount of emphasis we choose to put on a "dining" experience (as opposed to an "eating" experience) depends on the group demographics and the type of event.

Because food and drink inspire such strong emotional responses, everything connected to eating and drinking has the potential for a powerful impact, either positive or negative. This means that the kind and quality of food and drink we choose to offer participants matters. How the food

Encourage the chef to think big, and to have some fun with presentation.

is served during the event matters. How the food is displayed and presented before and during service matters. The amount of time that's allotted for eating matters. The options we offer to accommodate vegetarians, vegans, people with allergies, and people who don't drink alcohol – all of that matters, too. How the food is served, not to mention the ease with which our participants can actually eat it, matters. When it comes to food and drink, it all matters – and it all affects the design, execution, and perception of the event!

Food and Beverages

In food, as in so many other aspects of event planning, we must always be mindful of the tactical implications of meal planning, especially when we are sharing planning responsibilities with others – for instance, as part of a large conference or sponsorship involvement. I recall one conference where we ate chicken four meals in a row. Clearly the people responsible weren't communicating. What a lost opportunity!

Set the Right Expectations

I recently spoke at a conference where the catering department of the hotel was very excited about introducing a brand new luncheon menu. All of the attendees sat down for this new dining experience at tables of ten. Pre-set in the center of each table, like an eight-petal flower blossom, were huge platters of Tuscan-style salads, meats and a bountiful antipasto of cheese and vegetables. There were four platters on each side of each table. We all thought, "What a feast!" as we passed and piled the food, served ourselves, and went about enjoying what

PEOPLE WITH PEANUT ALERGIES NEED TO BE INFORMED THAT THE LAMB IN THIS DISH HAS BEEN COOKED IN **PEANUT OIL.**

To avoid potentially disastrous problems, we must be sure to discuss menus, timing, event schedule and serving options ahead of time. For instance: It doesn't matter how good the raw bar or the beef is, our guests can't consume only protein during a whole evening. They need a little balance, with some creative starches to absorb the alcohol they've been drinking, and they need a few vegetables. Similarly, we have the responsibility to know and understand the cultural tastes of our guests, and to offer a variety of options to appeal to everyone, from the vegans to the cattle barons.

Use famous faces as place cards. Give them something to talk about.

we thought was our complete meal, served family-style. Suddenly the waiter came to the table and asked whether we were aware this was the first course. No, we weren't aware!

Moments later, the second course of chicken and pasta materialized. Nobody ate much. Later, the Director of Catering and I discussed what had happened. The critical element, I realized, was presentation, display, and the size of our plates. They were full-sized, and they sent a clear visual message: "Fill me up." Had smaller plates and fewer platters been used, the message would have been a very different one: "Taste me – but save room for the next course." A printed menu, a creative sign, or some other enhancer could have provided the missing information and set the right expectations for attendees.

ENERGIZE YOUR EVENT: EXPERIMENT WITH TASTINGS

We've all heard of wine and cheese tasting events. Why stop there? Find a region-specific food or beverage that can tie into your event's main idea. Let's say that the theme of your event is "A World of Choices." All of the options below could help you to reinforce that theme with your group.

Coffee or Tea.

Offer five different blends of coffee and tea at breakfast – and orchestrate a coffee and tea-tasting. Have information about the history of the various coffees or teas being served. These cards also act as icebreakers; they give people something to talk about. (A side note: I am an ardent tea drinker, and will take advantage of virtually any opportunity to get properly brewed tea and an interesting tea selection onto the menu of an event.)

Seasonal Fruit

or other food that comes from the region where your venue is being held. For example, in Orlando, Florida, the exquisite Honeybell Tangelo and Honeybell Orange are available only once a year in early January. Put the history of these succulent fruits on the food station, offer samples of each, and treat them as the specialty they are.

Upscale Menu Items

that aren't region-specific. At receptions, you might reinforce a "Discover New Ways" theme by setting up tasting stations featuring sommeliers who can give your participants insights on any single gourmet food category of your choice: cheese, olives, honey, aged balsamic vinegar, mustard, butter, salt, pepper, dates and even asparagus! The possibilities are endless, interesting and educational.

Wine or Other Spirits

In addition to the ever popular wine tasting you could send your "World of Choices" message by staging a tasting event built around vodkas, tequilas, ports, champagnes, or liqueurs. Beer tastings have won great popularity in recent years. Have fun and get creative. A financial advisor I know hired an award-winning sommelier for an event called "Wining about Finances!" As you consider all of these options, you must, of course, bear in mind that not everyone drinks alcohol, so be certain to offer non-alcoholic options, mocktails and mocktinis for your guests. If you are in a part of the world where liquor consumption is a social taboo, you must find something else to build your tasting experience around.

For information on mixed drinks from the master mixologist in the industry, go to Dale DeGroff's web site **www.kingcocktail.com.**

Engage the senses of your group! Extend the idea of a "tasting" beyond the familiar wine and cheese ideas.

To encourage interaction, use a 'Lazy Susan" as a centerpiece to share condiments and promote conversation.

"Noncooks think it's silly to invest two hours' work in two minutes' enjoyment; but if cooking is evanescent, so is the ballet."
— Julia Child

THE ULTIMATE BRIDGE-BUILDER

Food is the ultimate bridge-builder ... so use it creatively to create connections among participants. You can sometimes find innovative ways to use food to engage the group, promote social interaction, and stretch a meager budget – all at the same time. One of my colleagues maximized a food budget by serving whole turkeys. On cue, waiters carried trays to each table. There was another surprise: The diner with a chef's hat under his chair won a set of cutlery, a carving knife and fork. This person also won the job of carving and serving the turkey! Interactive fun took over, and the budget did not have to accommodate the extra cost of having servers at each table. Since the theme was "Carving New Directions," the budget-friendly idea also supported the larger message the event was supposed to send.

Challenge yourself to use food creatively and interactively. Never stop asking good questions. For instance:

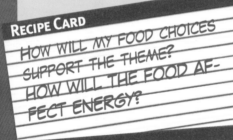

RECIPE CARD
HOW WILL MY FOOD CHOICES SUPPORT THE THEME? HOW WILL THE FOOD AFFECT ENERGY?

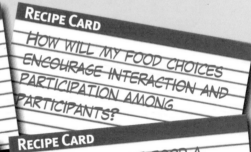

RECIPE CARD
HOW WILL MY FOOD CHOICES ENCOURAGE INTERACTION AND PARTICIPATION AMONG PARTICIPANTS?

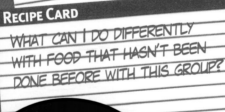

RECIPE CARD
WHAT CAN I DO DIFFERENTLY WITH FOOD THAT HASN'T BEEN DONE BEFORE WITH THIS GROUP?

RECIPE CARD
HOW CAN I MAKE FOOD A MORE PROMINENT FEATURE OF WHAT WE'RE ALL DOING TOGETHER?

RECIPE CARD
HOW CAN FOOD AND FOOD SERVICE AFFECT, SAY, AN AWARDS DINNER AND THE PRODUCTION ELEMENTS THAT ACCOMPANY IT?

Aside from the legal responsibilities associated with drinking at events, planners have the responsibility to meet the needs of people who do not drink alcohol for a variety of reasons. Added benefits to non-alcoholic beverages are their appeal to complement the theme, become part of the décor, distract from a premium bar, and appeal to everyone.

The solution:
Mocktails!

Arnold Palmer .... iced tea and lemonade.

Baptist Boilermaker .... a cup of coffee served with a glass of seltzer water.

Boston Cooler .... ginger ale and ice cream.

Faisal Ali .... 1 part orange juice, 1 part ginger ale, 1 part cranberry juice.

Cinderella .... 2 oz. Club Soda, 1 dash grenadine, 1 oz. lemon juice, orange juice, and pineapple juice.

Clayton .... ice, 1 nip Claytons, 1/2 a glass full of lemonade and 1/2 a glass full of ginger ale.

Nada Daiquiri .... A daiquiri made without any liquor

Dolce & Gabbana .... A drink consisting of diet Coke and grenadine syrup - named for its initials DC & G (However, this drink is also sometimes referred to as Roy Rogers).

Egg Cream .... chocolate syrup, milk, and seltzer

End Wrench .... 1 part orange juice, 1 part tonic water (This drink is also referred to as a Michelangelo)

Henry .... orange juice and lemonade.

Jeenie Juice .... a drink consisting of coke and passion fruit cordial.

Jefferson .... iced tea and orange juice.

Lemon, Lime & Bitters .... Has alcohol but the amount is so small and insignificant that it is usually classed as a mocktail.

Mock Champagne .... apple juice, ginger ale, and lemon juice or

2 liters ginger ale, 46 ounces pineapple juice and 64 ounces white grape juice or 4 parts carbonated water, 4 parts ginger ale and 3 parts white grape juice

Muddy Water .... cola and orange juice.

Pomme Noir .... apple juice and cola.

Roy Rogers ..... cola and grenadine syrup, garnished with a maraschino cherry.

Rebecca .... pineapple juice (1/3), cranberry juice (1/3), soda water (1/3).

Saint Clement's .... orange juice and a lemon-flavored drink.

Shirley Temple .... Ginger ale and grenadine syrup.

Virgin Mary .... a Bloody Mary without the vodka.

Virgin Caesar .... a Bloody Caesar without the vodka.

Virgin Piña Colada .... coconut cream, and pineapple juice

Virgin Mint Julep .... made with Crème de menthe and Limeade; often served at Disneyland in New Orleans Square.

Both mocktails and cocktails can cross the line into décor. Serve them through a luge attached to a custom ice bar or in distinctive glassware. By choosing serving pieces creatively, you can maximize the effect of one specialty spirit!

"An effective event marketing campaign includes six to eight touch points to reach prospective guests and attendees. What mix is used is based on the event and the variable elements involved."

COLLATERAL

You are Invited!

are

ted!

invite you to experience
KashMir
Oh may the SUN
shine upon my face with STARS to fill my dreams
I am a wanderer through TIME and SPACE
to be where I must go
Let me take you there
Let me take you there
ElectricFactory
MONDAY, JANUARY 9, 2006
Let us take
Date
Monday, January 9, 2006
Location
Electric Factory
421 North Seventh Street
Philadelphia PA
Time
9pm – 1am
RSVP @ www.dndgroup.com/kashmir
Please register for transportation details.
Finder File Edit View Go Window Help

Diannizing

COLLATERAL

Every event actually begins before it physically begins. The marketing collateral that supports the event represents the first "touch" with the participant, and thus represents the true beginning of the live "face meet."

Collateral includes, among other things, the following: a custom graphic, a save-the-date announcement, a formal invitation, web notification, e-mail updates, social media messaging, and all follow-up evaluations, messages and interaction after the event. (Thus, good collateral can ensure that the meeting actually never "ends" either – even after it physically ends!)

It should be no surprise how important marketing and promotion is in determining the success or failure of an event. The supporting materials used in meetings and events, and particularly the invitations, are very likely to be "make-or-break" elements in your campaign ... and they're particularly important if you're trying to generate interest, increase attendance, and affirm buy-in for a complex event. Collateral plays a critical role in the three different stages of every event: pre-event, on-site during the event, and follow-up after the event. There should be a single unifying element that brands all three into a unified, appealing whole.

Good collateral sets expectations. Collateral must give a sense of the environment we are creating. It must evoke the world we're inviting people to enter, and it must inspire them to want to connect with that world. It must engage the emotions of everyone who encounters it, concisely support your theme, and preview the larger message of the gathering. Before it can do any of those things, however, *your collateral must stand out.*

MAKE IT SING!

Your collateral must sing to everyone who encounters it. By "sing," I mean that your collateral must become something intriguing, a beckoning message, a seductive song that creates interest and engagement, and inspire a specific action on the part of the person who encounters it: checking out a web site, returning an RSVP, marking the calendar, whatever response is prompted. It's certainly possible to make a powerful initial impression with collateral on a modest investment, but with many high-profile events that have long lead times and lots of competition for attention, it's quite possible a respectable portion of the budget will be allocated to collateral. Regardless of how much is spent, you must ensure that the collateral supports the theme, and that it works in coordination with the other elements of your plan.

The supporting materials used in meetings and events, and particularly the invitations, are likely to be "make-or-break" elements in the event marketing campaign.

Images: Alpine Creative Group

MAKE A PROMISE

All collateral that participants encounter before the event, and particularly collateral that takes the form of an invitation, is a promise about good things that will happen. It's important to keep all the promises you make in the invitation. One major hotel company promised guests "An evening filled with surprises" if they attended the gathering the hotel was hosting. Upon arriving at an industrial area in Los Angeles, guests were escorted into a building that had, at one time, apparently been a swimming pool. None of the waiters or staff knew the building's history, or why we were all gathered around the perimeter. When the hosts appeared, they advised us that we were standing in what had, 70 years earlier, been an elite Hollywood health club used by the Cary Grants of the world. That was the sum total of the "surprises" that we had been promised would fill our evening! That information was not a surprise; it was history. With a different (and more accurate) promise, the historic nature of the site could have been used effectively in the marketing collateral with a period photo and a good description of what we were actually going to experience when we showed up! As it was, all the attendees – including yours truly – felt let down – and the event lost an opportunity to make an impression that it would never have again.

The supporting materials used in meetings and events, and particularly the invitations, are very likely to be "make-or-break" elements in your campaign.

Images: Alpine Creative Group, NYC

The collateral sent a powerful message: You have been invited because you matter to us.

SAVE THE DATE AND INVITATIONS – TO HAVE AND TO HOLD?

These elements must correlate directly to all the other elements in your marketing plan, including such pieces as web site pages, print ads, press releases, and public service announcements. They are the first "ads" for the event.

"Save the date" messages and invitations are meant to create a dialogue by sending a message and asking for a response. Keep their design clear, spare, and simple: include information about day, date, time, place, dress code, and parking. Lots of graphics and text may divert the recipient's attention from the purpose, which is the action item related to attending the event. You want the person to either mark the calendar or send you an RSVP, or both. These pieces require action. Consider the following true story!

One of my clients was hosting an Oscar Night themed event. The objective of the event was to introduce the new management team to their top one hundred customers – an elite group of major players. I knew that the priority objective was for people to attend. We had to design a powerful, personalized first impression with the invitation if we wanted to reach this level.

Ask yourself, "what percentage of the preprinted mail that you receive from someone you don't recognize do you discard unopened?" For most of us, that percentage is about 90%. The group being targeted was likely to push that 90% number up to 99%. The problem was, we couldn't afford a ninety-nine percent discard rate with these one hundred customers ... so we had to invest in creating, designing, and delivering this important piece of collateral.

The Oscar Night invite was delivered via overnight courier. Upon opening the FedEx box, the addressee saw a beautiful hand-addressed 5"x10" gold envelope lined in black. The name was addressed on an outside card, and featured hand-executed calligraphy. Consider this: The addressee's name was executed in beautiful calligraphy. To open the envelope, the addressee had to break an old-fashioned wax seal. The two engraved cards inside informed the person that he or she had been "nominated" to attend the upcoming event, and gave all the details including an overnight stay and spa treatment. Each and every step experienced as you engaged with that piece of collateral — opening the FedEx box, seeing the unique shape of the envelope, feeling the paper, seeing your name in hand-written calligraphy, breaking the wax seal—all counted as "touch points" that established top-of- mind expectations for that event. Far from a 99% discard rate, the result was 99% attendance — with many of the guests offering to send a superior based on the quality of the invitation if they personally could not attend. The collateral sent a powerful message: *You have been invited because you matter to us.* It also presented an impossible-to-forget Visual Dynamic that supported the theme.

Today's evites and other virtual announcements have their place, but I believe that "hard copy" invitations, such as the one we used for the Oscar Night event, will always have their place, too.

Effective marketing collateral provides multiple communication "touches." A powerful invitation, for instance, uses multiple elements – paper, text, delivery mode – to deliver a great first impression for the event, and to build anticipation. The paper (not needed if talking about texture), size, look, style, texture, layout, font, and design used in pre-event marketing collateral is the precursor, the first act of the play, the overture of a symphony that must be carried through on-site signage, banners, presentations, and theme décor– in and on nearly everything, to be an effective business communication tool. This is the live "advertisement" that establishes expectations and builds anticipation.

The save-the-date and invitation accounted for 38% of the budget for this event, which is extremely high ... but that investment allowed us to accomplish a critical objective: getting people to show up. This was a great example of effective use of budget priorities to maximize Return on Event.

We live in a wired world, and that means to a great extent the marketing collateral we create is going to be experienced on the internet. Considering how much registration and other vital pre-event information can be exchanged online now, most participants will expecting their first interaction with you to be virtual, while others will still expect invitations via old-fashioned snail mail. Gear the collateral to the expectations of the audience, and prepare multiple versions if necessary.

SIGN ME UP!

There are many registration programs on the market today; in evaluating them, you should remember the old saying, "You get what you pay for." I tell my classes the story of a restaurant in New York City that advertises French Fries for $19.95 *. The asterisk denotes that the fries come with filet mignon. When it comes to online registration programs, it's fine to order the fries, but consider a package that includes filet mignon.

Most times, planners do not have all the program details and clarity on goals at the starting point and what the needs will be in the end, i.e. additional programs added, directions to venue, logistics. Most importantly, these programs have and are best utilized when they collect data upfront that can be used during the event and in post-event marketing. By not identifying event and program content upfront and having unknowns, it is challenging to customize a site in the beginning with the main goal of having the program work efficiently for you in the end. *Begin with the end in mind.* This component is critical in all the phases of pre-event, on-site, and post-event experience by allowing you to integrate the entire marketing and promotion campaign, communication with attendees, data management; social media, and sponsor opportunities along with advertising the message, theme and visuals.

Use of the internet for registration purposes spills over to e-marketing, reports, collecting payments and a whole host of other functions.

The internet, and specifically, today's social media networks, allow us to build meetings and events that never end. These tools are game-changers, and we will continue to adapt to them and benefit from their use and application by asking good questions.

What information will we need to gather from participants in order to plan the event? How should we gather that information and store it? What facts or assignments do people need to have ahead of time? What do we need to ask up front, as they register, that will help us to gather, identify, and provide useful post-event marketing statistics?

As you ponder such questions, remember that it is much more efficient for a programmer (or whoever is developing your data management system) to build a mansion that can be populated with data than it is to try to stuff everything into a one-room apartment. This is not simply a matter of building a site experience that correlates to and supports your theme. You want to build something that is functional, easy to navigate, and provides important logistical details upfront without having to search for them. As if all that weren't enough, you want the online experience insofar as possible to be effortless.

Use of the internet for registration purposes spills over to e-marketing, reports, collecting payments and a whole host of other functions. It's not surprising that the design of such a system takes time, resources, and a careful, logical approach. If your budget permits, and if the event is large enough to

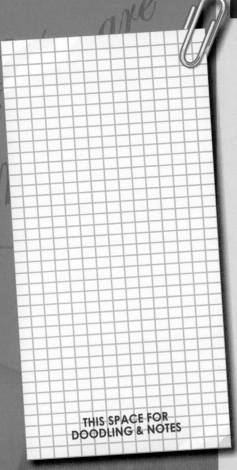

THIS SPACE FOR
DOODLING & NOTES

warrant it, a prudent investment in information systems can end up being one of the best budget decisions. Just remember that *the system must support the event needs, not determine them.*

All the data you gather during the event should serve as the "fuel" for your post-event marketing. Put it to work quickly. If you don't use this information, you will lose it!

The type of registration system and use of the internet is based on the individual situation and specific needs. Many companies have internal, customized programs that do the job of announcing a meeting and requesting a response.

Events that require inviting and attracting the public have different objectives – no two are alike. Make sure you understand the support that comes with the software program you use, or have a trained professional on your team dedicated to managing this fundamental and critical component of the event. Do not attempt to do this alone if you are not experienced. All the information involved with online registration, marketing, save-the-date messaging, invitations, and similar virtual collateral must be created and transmitted in a way that concisely supports the overall theme. Do not use the registration process as an excuse to deliver program content to the participants. Keep your message simple, clear, and factual. Focus on what's in it for them if they attend.

"Singing is to speaking what dancing is to walking." – **Arthur Samuel Joseph,** *Founder Vocal Awareness*

MUSIC & ENTERTAINMENT

Diannizing

MUSIC & ENTERTAINMENT

Music is such a central part of the human experience that it's hard to imagine our world without it. When the 9/11 attack occurred, the sudden lack of music was one of the first signals to me that a major change had taken place, and that something about the city where I lived would never be the same. Suddenly the bustling, vibrant, loud streets were disturbingly silent. What I realized that day was that the lack of music, too, confirms something essential about who we are as people. We notice when music is absent, just as we notice the silence after a new snowstorm. Today, the Amtrak terminal at Penn Station plays easy listening and classical music — as compared to the pre 9/11 choice to play loud, contemporary music. The behavior of travelers in the terminal is noticeably more subdued.

"Music and rhythm find their way into the secret places of the soul"
— Plato quotes (Ancient Greek Philosopher He was the world's most influential philosopher. 428 BC-348 BC)

Learning cannot take place when there is a perceived threat, and music is great tool for establishing a sense of safety in the event space.

Music has a profound effect on attitude, motivation, and behavior. Stanford University held a symposium in 2006 that focused on the therapeutic benefits of music and rhythm, and explored the correlation of music to brainwave activity. The scientists recognized that music, whether it expresses itself in strong beats or gentle rhythms, has a direct link to brainwave stimulation, and can have a positive effect on reaction time, awareness, and the ability to focus and concentrate with acute awareness. Music can also help us to slow down; it can promote calm, a sense of ease, and a more meditative state – all of which opens the brain to learning.

Learning cannot take place when there is a perceived threat, and music is great tool for establishing a sense of safety in the event space.

In 1993, the Center for the Neurobiology of Learning and Memory at the University of California, Irvine, gave college students IQ-related spatial-reasoning tests three times after either listening to Mozart's Sonata for Two Pianos in D Major, listening to 10 minutes of relaxation instructions designed to lower the blood pressure, or sitting in silence for 10 minutes. Their IQ scores averaged eight to nine points higher after listening to Mozart than under the other two conditions."

"Musicians and mystics have long recognized the power of rhythmic music. Ritual drumming and rhythmic prayer are found in cultures throughout the world and are used in ceremonies to induce trance states. There is a growing body of neuroscientists who support the theory that if there's a physical correlate of conscious experience, it has to be happening in the brainwaves. It seems to be the only thing in your head that changes rapidly enough to explain real-time changes in consciousness."

Stanford University Press Release
– Emily Saarman, May 2006

Music, much like color, is a language unto itself, and its deeply ritualized appeal to the human memory has no parallel.

We have all had the experience of hearing a song that immediately brings back total, instant recall of where we were, who we were with, and sometimes even what we were wearing when the song was played. This is because music offers the potential of an extraordinary rejuvenating effect on everyone who comes in contact with it; it offers instant recall about exactly who we were and exactly how we felt in our body at a certain specific time in our lives.

One of my industry colleagues, producer Jeremy Driesen, calls this effect the "16/25 Rule," and his rule is worthy of close study by any event designer looking for a secret to instant success. According to Jeremy (and my own personal experience), every time you expose a participant to music he or she heard between the ages of sixteen and twenty-five, you allow that participant to become the age at which the music was first heard. This fact carries astonishing implications. You can, if you wish, transport participants back to a time when the dance floor was full, their personalities were still forming, and all was possible. Try it!

Learning cannot take place when there is a perceived threat, and music is great tool for establishing a sense of safety in the event space.

Try playing some disco music when you're feeling down. Notice how it elevates your mood. Music really is the second best medicine (after laughter)!

The field of Music Therapy uses music to prevent and manage chronic stress and promote goodmental health.

Supporting the Well-Planned Event

Although music and entertainment are two distinct disciplines, their value and application are the same. It is when, where, why, and how to use each, that magnify their individual appeal and impact. After all, music is entertainment and entertainment can be music. Don't forget the power of professional speakers to motivate, stimulate, inspire, educate, and enforce the message and theme as meeting entertainment.

Music and entertainment support the well-planned event. They:

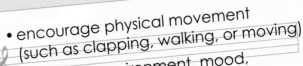
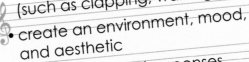

- encourage physical movement (such as clapping, walking, or moving)
- create an environment, mood, and aesthetic
- evoke emotional responses (sometimes quite powerful ones)
- promote well-being through cognitive and mental processes
- evoke a sense of connection to a Higher Power
- are social meet the needs of both individuals and groups
- unite people
- promote interaction and communication
- can support the theme(s) you have chosen
- are just plain fun and support permission to Go Play!

Music and entertainment are practical tools that can be used to manage and control movement and tempo, two important factors in any event. Often, groups have to transition from one floor to another, one space to another, one building to another, or even one moment to another in the same room. The creative elements of music and entertainment allow the planner and the producer plenty of options for timing, executing, and synchronizing these events – as well as the opportunity to tie them to the chosen theme. When a musician or entertainer is placed at strategic points during these transitions, guests and attendees are distracted by the show; for the moment, they literally forget the inconvenience of having to physically move from one place to another.

Performers can be used as directional "human arrows," or can physically lead attendees from one point to another. (You can outfit performers with dress and costume choices that complement the theme to add personality and pizzazz.) Sometimes the music itself is powerful enough to guide participants to the action the designer has in mind. At an annual beach concert I know of in New Jersey, the band always concludes with a marching song. The high-spirited music encourages fast movement — and effectively disburses the crowd of over 5,000 in less than an hour!

Music and Entertainment as Kinetic Engineering Tools

At a private corporate awards event produced years ago in Las Vegas, the challenge was time. There were over 40 awards to be given out after the 1600-plus guests enjoyed dinner. The older, unionized wait staff were used to serving meals "the way we always do it." The goal: speed up the service without affecting the guest's experience. To make this happen, we brought in a professional choreographer to work with the senior wait staff. Between each course, the wait staff came out, stood at their stations and waited for a different down-tempo song (such as "Bolero") to begin. Each server performed a unique "routine," carrying trays and serving the guests in time with the music. The guests became involved and enjoyed the transitions, and the classical music kept the tempo and temperaments under control. A four-course meal was served in an hour and a half — without any complaints!

Image: Pink Inc.

It's possible that the location of your event has a natural tie-in to music and/or entertainment. If you choose a destination or theme an event around a destination, consider working your theme around the powerful associations people will already have with that destination.

• New Orleans (Jazz)
• St. Louis (Blues)
• Chicago (Blues)
• Nashville (Country-Western)
• New York (Broadway)
• Los Angeles (Movies)
• Ashland, Oregon (Shakespeare)

On an international note, there is a spectacular annual festival in Tallinn, Estonia that features music from over 20 countries. *www.tallinnmusicweek.ee.*

Whatever the budget, you can find a way to inspire your participants with one musician or several as the impact will be the same. You will always give people something in common, something they can talk about. No other medium transcends all borders and reaches all people the way music does.

Entertainment choices range from "A-list" celebrities, headline talent, tribute bands, comedians and dancers to walk-around performers and novelty acts. Whatever and whoever is the most in demand in popular entertainment is always a guideline on what will be in demand for events. Alternatively, there are some wonderful acts that are built exclusively for events. The possibilities are endless – just make sure that the choice you make is driven by the theme and strategic intent of the event.

Serious meetings can make use of music by incorporating a musician at the breaks, registration or in room transitions. Work with a professional agent or a Strategic Event Designer and producer who can make creative suggestions that will help you to choose your live entertainment. There are many "no names" out there that have fabulous acts and are budget friendly. If you don't work with professionals, you risk what quality standards he or she will reflect. I once hired a top-of-the-line Cher look-a-like; en route, she was in a car accident. A substitute was sent, but based on her costume and looks, I refused to let her on stage. It wasn't worth the risk. Professionals will know how to book the event, what legalities are involved, and how to negotiate terms. There are many details and options – don't take a risk.

STEP BACK IN TIME.

One of the first events that taught me the power of contrast and surprise using music and entertainment was an indoor beach party theme called "Good Vibrations." Guests were informally dancing to DJ music, wearing flip-flops and enjoying food like hot dogs and burgers. At a well-orchestrated time, when the attendees were in high density dancing mode, a "reveal" took place around the DJ. A curtained wall opened and suddenly, there were the actual Beach Boys, playing the same song as the DJ. You can imagine the reaction of the group as one by one they realized what had happened! You can do this kind of thing, too, on any scale budget. *Remember, it's the emotion, the surprise, the unexpected that will create the memory.*

Does the event need the pulsing points of energy that a living artist, stilt walker, or spectacle performer can provide? If the event is historical, can a period actor be used to greet and speak with guests or make an announcement onstage? How could you use a human "event energizer" to create the perfect first impression?

Music and entertainment should create vivid first and last impressions. "Walk-in" music should be themed; choose it carefully. What is the first visual impression a performer can provide? What energy level should this be? What your guests see and hear as they begin to engage with the live experience will affect their ability to retain, and act on the message. Similarly, the last experience that takes place as part of the live event – and particularly the last song your participants hear – carries special power. Like the song says, "You have to know when to fold them." When you "feel" energy at its peak, trust that intuition to "know" when to stop the music and let that last impression be something your guests can "take home."

Work with the musicians when planning the flow and staggering the breaks, and remember that too much of any entertainer can be as disastrous an effect as too little.

THE ART OF DEPLOYING TALENT

Deploy your live "talent" strategically to create a seamless experience, build energy and maximize the effect. When engaging a band, I often hire additional musicians and rotate and stagger them to maximize impact. I assign one or two of them to greet guests, and another one or two (or more) to play in a reception area; then, at a predetermined time, everyone joins the main band or orchestra on stage.

Certain events need to have continuous music and entertainment. For these events, there should be no dead spots. This raises a logistical challenge: If you are working with live performers, they need breaks. When the band plays for 40 minutes and suddenly stops, the energy, the flow and the entire event are affected by the sudden sound of silence; the room is emotionally empty. Work with the musicians when planning the flow and staggering the breaks. Remember, also, that in some situations, too much of any novelty entertainer can be as disastrous an effect as too little. You may be able to use a specialty musician for as little as five minutes to provide the needed effect.

MATCH THE ENTERTAINMENT TO THE GROUP ... AND THE VENUE

You must make sure the entertainment you select is appropriate for group and the environment. That definitely includes volume levels. The music and entertainment choices you make must match the scale of the space in which you are holding the event. Sometimes, the space changes unexpectedly, and you must make rapid adjustments to the kind of entertainment you offer.

For weeks, I had been planning a major, high-budget event that was to be held in a huge ballroom in New York City. The production included a runway-style stage and performers wearing dramatic colorful costumes with a wing span of about twenty feet side. Some of these costumes were fifteen feet tall. Obviously, this was to be a spectacle. One week before the event, the hotel received a phone call that the mayor's office wanted to use the ballroom we had booked on the night of the event. With only days to go before the event, we were moved to a room with a ten-foot-high ceiling. So much for my entertainment plan and its super-sized costume! Our talent changed from one version of grand spectacle to another, as we substituted the massively-garbed entertainers with a parade of fabulously costumed drag queens singing, performing, and engaging the group to dance. The element of surprise would be hard to surpass

The event was a huge success – low ceilings and all. Remember: You become the director of a special kind of play when you start planning and producing an event. Music and entertainment are the essential tools that allow you to engage with your participants, tell your story, and deliver the message. Use your palette!

We live in an multimedia era, and so do our participants. The days of one-dimensional events and meetings are – or, at least should be — over.

PRODUCTION

Furniture: PPG

Diannizing

TECHNICAL PRODUCTION

The final category to consider is Technical Production, including multimedia technology. What I am focusing on here specifically are the three aspects of any "show" that deliver a level of professionalism in the meeting and event and reinforce the message. These elements are:

AUDIO VISUAL

LIGHTING

STAGING

I believe these elements must be used to serve a single, essential goal: To keep the audience focused, attentive and listening to the message. Think of a Presidential message being delivered on television, or a breaking news story, or a rock concert or your Chairman being videotaped for a webcast. In each case, there are visual theatrics that give the speaker and the message credibility for the intended audience, and keep the audience engaged.

The word "production" has many connotations in the me ings and events industry. In a strict sense, everything at the meeting or event is part of a production.

In previous chapters, we have discussed "Choosing the Colors," and have focused on the importance of deliberate design choices in décor, food and beverage, marketing collateral, music and entertainment. The choices made in each of these areas should also drive the productions decisions that will determine the visual dynamics, the kinetic engineering, and the branding of the event.

Arthur Samuel Joseph, founder of Vocal Awareness, and an internationally acknowledged expert on voice and sound, notes in his book Vocal Power that in any physical, face-to-face presentation, the message comes from three sources.

8% of the message comes from the words themselves;

37% of the message comes from things like vocal tones, inflections, and volume;

55% of the message comes from physical mannerisms – posture, expressions, eye contact, and the way the speaker's face looks under lighting. So, if ninety-two percent of any speaker's communication involves something other than the words chosen for a speech, it stands to reason that the way that speaker is presented plays a major role in the success or failure of the message.

Production values have escalated in importance in recent years, so much so that the leading production companies in the industry that they are now referred to as Brand Communication Agencies, Communication Agencies, or by similar titles. This evolution will continue, paralleling meeting and event professionals as titles change and they become builders, architects, strategic event designers. Whatever names are used, the production experience breaks down into the use of these essential areas of expertise: audiovisual, lighting, and staging.

AUDIO VISUAL

Audiovisual production ("AV" for short) encompasses any and all choices the event designer makes that connect to a visual or auditory experience the participant has during the event. The source can be either live or recorded. Audio Visual elements, like everything else connected to the event, must always support the theme, objectives and goals we're promoting; they must do so in a way that focuses the attention of the entire group. Let me share an example of what I mean.

At a recent memorial event I produced for a global luminary who had passed away (I'll call him Mr. Murray), all the production choices, and the AV choices in particular, were critical to the impact of the event. In creating a theme for this event, I met with the family and discussed numerous details about Mr. Murray's life. I wasn't so interested in what was public and newsworthy – but rather what was personal to the man.

I discovered that he liked music from the 1940s, yellow roses, and yachting. These elements served as the inspiration for the "walk-in" music that played as people arrived; they was also the impetus for the opening entertainer, who sang "I'll Be Seeing You," a popular song from the World War II years, and one which Mr. Murray particularly loved. The stage had accents of yellow roses, and the slide show included personal photos of the boating trips Mr. Murray and his family cherished. During the change of speakers, short video clips (known as interstitials) reinforced the themes of each attendee's special relationship to Mr. Murray. The AV choices helped to make the event a completely integrated experience.

How much less effective would the event have been if the songs and images had been chosen by someone who didn't understand – or know about – the guiding theme of personal relationships?

"Research has shown that boredom is closely related to frustration and that the effect of too much frustration is invariably irritability, withdrawal, rebellious opposition or aggressive rejection of the whole show." – Fritz Redl

We live in an multimedia era, and so do our participants. The days of one-dimensional events and meetings are – or at least should be — over.

We live in a multimedia era, and so do our participants. The days of one-dimensional events and meetings are, or at least should be over. People are now comparing our event content to content they receive via the internet, from their video games, films, and from their high-definition televisions – all of which are likely to be simultaneously in use, at any given moment. The term "integrated marketing" has spilled over into all areas of technology, enabling cross-blending technology, interactive experience and social media.

As a result, there is no "simple corporate meeting" anymore. We have a responsibility to appeal to the multi-screen, multi-element, perpetual-stimulus audience. All meetings and events are communication messages – messages that build brands and increase brand awareness – and we have a professional responsibility to offer multiple sources of AV stimulation for any and every gathering. What's more, we have an obligation to ensure the quality and standards of the AV content are high.

Perhaps the most important (or at least the most commonly overlooked) of these elements is sound.

It's frighteningly easy to lose your audience because of a poor sound setup. "Music to your ears" definitely does not include loud, shrill static, or uncontrolled volume experience. If sound is not designed and balanced properly in a given space; if it is not based on the unique needs of the meeting or event production; then the result is not going to be harmonious and inviting for your participants. Instead, it is going to be like fingernails across a blackboard. Sound engineers know they can manage and control the sound output by using different types of speakers and placing them strategically to adjust to the acoustic realities of the space based on the presentation or performance. How, when, and where these speakers are best placed are complex design decisions with far-reaching impacts and the event's success or failure very often depends on how they are made.

NO SUCH THING AS "HOUSE SOUND"

Many venues and hotels will advise you that they have built-in sound setups, "house sound," or "distributed sound." Despite what you may be told, these systems were not designed for your specific VIP speaker, rock concert, or gospel group performance. They were designed for "house" announcements, such as fire drills and emergency notifications. They do not allow for any design, management, or control.

Most club environments, by contrast, have sophisticated sound systems for music — but not for business speakers. Work with a professional, and don't assume that the sound system you inherit is the required sound system. The professionals will guide you on things like power requirements, the risks you face, and available options or solutions. A good sound engineer will make adjustments for each individual or group that is participating as part of a large event production during the essential sound check prior to the event. This means getting people to rehearse with the sound engineer before the event to set levels. Why bother with this? Because each speaker's natural tone, pitch, and cadence is going to be different, and sound design must accommodate those differences. The same goes for the live entertainment: the meeting and event planner cannot simply hire a band without augmenting the performance with proper sound equipment and doing a sound check ahead of time.

Don't subject your participants to the dreaded "Is this thing on?" moment when a hesitant speaker taps on a microphone.

How, when, and where speakers are best placed are complex decisions with far-reaching impacts. The event's success or failure very often depends on how these decisions are made.

Prepare, and rehearse, until you and your presenters or entertainers are comfortable operating in a balanced sound environment that can support music and messaging.

Sometimes, the disastrous effects of poor sound engineering only express themselves on a subliminal level. The result: Participants miss about 20% of what they're supposed to be getting, and thus don't quite connect with the speaker or talent. They assume that they've been subjected to a "bad speaker" or a "bad band." Actually, they've been subjected to a bad sound experience, but they didn't realize it.

Arthur Samuel Joseph often reiterates "We remember under 15% of what we hear. If that message is disrupted because of ineffective sound, an opportunity is lost forever."

EVERY SPACE IS UNIQUE
No two spaces you will work in are identical, which means no two spaces will have the same AV requirements. Effective AV design will take into account the height of the ceilings, the columns, the windows, the chandeliers, draping, the flooring (is it marble or carpet?), the number of people attending the event, and any number of other essential architectural details unique to the location. Sound design must not only take into account the acoustics of the venue – it must also take into account whether there is another event taking place nearby simultaneously. If there is, you'd better find out what type of event is going to be taking place in the room next door. What if the Blue Man Group is supposed to be performing at the same time a tribute speech is to be given during the memorial service you are planning?

AN UNDER-UTILIZED TOOL

I believe audiovisual is the most constantly underutilized tool on the meeting planners' palette. Why? Perhaps because we avoid and minimize the value of whatever we're not familiar with. Many planners are intimidated by equipment, mechanical problems, and unfamiliar technical terms that could influence wrong decisions. So they simply disengage. Here's a question: What happens if we take the same approach with our cars? Disaster! When there's a problem with our car, we take the car to the right mechanic and trust he or she knows what to fix. I personally don't know what motor mounts are, but I assume they are important. If a mechanic I have reason to trust tells me that they need to be fixed, they are going to get fixed. When it comes to AV, we must learn to defer to the expertise of outsourced production professionals. If we don't, we court disaster.

This leads us to a larger point that connects to successful technical production: *The biggest responsibility a planner owns is the judgment to do whatever is needed to minimize risk.* I've had students tell me they "don't have budgets" for back up equipments at an important meeting for a gathering of executives at a Fortune 1000 company. That's an AV disaster waiting to happen. There simply is no excuse for not educating stakeholders about exactly what is needed to get the job done and to minimize the possibility of "event trauma." This education about what is necessary for effective risk management is peace of mind. It is good planning. It is insurance. It is non-negotiable.

Before hiring an outside company to help you with AV design and execution, take time to understand the capabilities of the company you are considering working with. Ask what they have done in the past, and compare their experience to what you want them to do now. Choose someone who will help you to plan effectively and avoid problems.

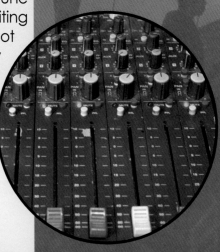

"Light is not so much something that reveals, as it is itself the revelation." —James Turrell

A colleague who worked at a major entertainment conglomerate was responsible for planning an all-employee Town Hall meeting. The Chairman of the company was at the podium speaking in front of 1000 employees — when suddenly the sound went dead. No one could hear a word. Tension mounted in the silence during the two very long minutes that it took to fix the problem.

Why did this messaging catastrophe take place? Because someone had neglected to be prepared with a back-up microphone check!

PRODUCTION: LIGHTING

Color is Light and Light is Energy

Ask any artist or designer about the properties of lighting and you will hear one common answer: Natural lighting, caught at just the precise moment of intensity, is unsurpassed in quality. It changes the intensity and color of whatever it touches. Unfortunately, event designers don't always have access to natural light, and so must create substitutes for it.

Lighting designers and technicians are descendants of a long chain of professionals who have searched for those substitutes. In the European theatre, a lighting revolution began in the fifteenth century with the use of oil lamps for indoor productions. These lamps were treated with red wine or colored glass to control the design. There were lighting or stage assistants who would 'trim the wicks' of the

Image: Alex Fogel Lighting Design.
The Winston-Salem Lighting Project 2008.

candles to manage the amount of light emanating from one source. Theatrical lighting continued to progress through the 19th century, eventually using a system of "dips and floats" where fully lit candelabras were lowered onto the stage for full lighting effects, or candles "floated" in a trough at the front edge, or apron of the stage – the precursors of modern-day footlights. We owe the term "limelight" to theatre origins, to a time when the "spotlight" effect we now take for granted relied on lime (not the green kind, the toxic kind) mixed with hydrogen and oxygen. It made for a big impression!

Needless to say, the use of lime, oil, kerosene, and lit candles presented a bit of a safety hazard in many of the original wooden theatre structures, to say nothing of the smoke and fumes the audiences experienced in the closed environment. The next time you are in a theatre, be aware of this evolution. It marked the beginning of the production industry that is the contemporary "business theatre" of meetings and events.

LET THERE BE LIGHT!

The foremost purpose of lighting is illumination. Effective and dramatic illumination must support the theme, and must also take into account factors like environment, mood, control, timing, and décor. An astute lighting designer knows how to use all of these elements to enhance the meeting and event experience, and to direct the attention of participants so that they focus on a certain place or person. They can trick the eye into believing that a space is larger than it really is by using cunning effects in a low-ceilinged room, and they can add energy and drama to particularly important moments. Even the greatest lighting designer, however, can't work in a vacuum. The producer and designer must let the lighting designer know exactly what the participants should be paying attention to in the first place. Like all the other stakeholders on the planner's palette, lighting designers need

The power of lighting derives from knowing what to accent and when and where it should be accented.

to know all the details of the meeting and event, including all printed collateral, décor, colors, floor plans, and the event production schedule.

The field of professional lighting is evolving rapidly, with a stunning array of new technologies introduced on an almost daily basis. The use of LEDs, fiber optics, and other wireless devices are enabling the industry to create new products and effects with dazzling speed, efficiency, and flexibility. "Lighting" your event can now mean illuminated walls and floors, illuminated furniture, illuminated linens, and even illuminated clothing, each of which can send a message that adds to an event's impact. Today's lighting instruments include colored gels that can create specific effects. Modern computerized equipment can be programmed to deliver an exact hue, using the thousands of colors represented in the Pantone color series. Gobos or stencil forms can now be projected on anything — floors, walls, buildings, and streets – to create instant décor.

Today's state-of-the-art lighting equipment doesn't require wires or cables, can be positioned virtually anywhere, can be controlled remotely, and can be programmed to provide thin beams of light to accent, for instance, a table centerpiece. Just as Hollywood uses searchlights to announce a premiere, we can use lighting to draw attention to a specific place where something special is happening ... or about to happen. Modern lighting allows us to create an environment including "chandeliers" and "furniture" to enhance a space – all with computer technology or through the use of gobos – a shadow outline of anything projected through light.

Creating such dazzling effects, however, requires an understanding of all the variables in play: power source, ceiling height, size of room, the architecture in the room, the setup time needed, and, of course, the budget. Just as with sound, we can enhance the experience by working with experienced lighting professionals. These are the people who can eliminate unwanted shadows from the face of your main speaker, illuminate a low-ceilinged room, help with color effects, and add energy and drama to particularly important moments. Working with them will make the unique properties of the event space support your message.

There are dramatic differences between "theatrical event" lighting and the types of lighting used to create décor. Like any category of hardware, lighting equipment comes in varying styles customized for a specific use. An experienced professional will know to choose the right tool for the right moment based on many factors including budget, venue size, distances, program, power, etc.

One VIP event I worked on took place in a converted airplane hanger, and was powered by a stand-alone generator. Just at the moment the President approached the stage and began speaking —the highlight of the evening — the lights went out. Fortunately, backup lights went on almost immediately, and the speaker made a joke of the situation. The reason for the problem was that the no one had bothered to check the fuel level of the sub-contracted generator. No, we don't have to be experts on things like stand-alone generators ... but we do have to make sure we're working with someone who is an expert, and who is capable of putting together a backup plan that incorporates the best of the "old ways" and the new technologies. Add it to the checklist.

Image: Ira Levy Lighting NYC

Another simple (and cost-effective) trick involves an old friend, the disco ball, or a mirror ball, illuminated and suspended from a ceiling.

LIGHTING TRICKS: OLDIES BUT GOODIES

One of my favorite low-budget lighting tricks is to place six to eight votive or self-lit candles on top of a round mirror or square tile in the center of a table. The glow from the candles reflects light from the mirror — giving an effect similar to a pin spot.

Another simple (and cost-effective) trick involves an old friend, the disco ball, or a mirror ball, illuminated and suspended from a ceiling. If you think disco balls are completely "out," don't forget that they remain an amazingly effective and inexpensive way to transform a space on a low budget by illuminating the ceiling and walls and, if on a motor, can provide s-l-o-w movement.

PRODUCTION: STAGING

Staging in theatre (and meetings and events are theatre!) means drawing attention to any area that is a focal point in the production, and de-emphasizing other areas. It is the art of directing attention.

Staging also refers to the overall look, blocking, placement, and movement of elements and people who perform on the stage. The elements of set design, from drapes to lights, to the platforms people stand on, all fall under the staging umbrella. Based on the location, the venue, and the event, the stage we use may be custom designed, may be part of the venue (and thus built in a specific style), or may be rented in various configurations.

What physical staging format should you choose? The format you choose must complement the act, the event, and the performer's needs – and must maximize the attendee experience. The physical space in which the event takes place will help to determine your final choice.

I have often featured a popular act called "Dueling Pianos." It features two pianists playing with, for, and against each other, to the audience's inevitable delight. Rather than use one rectangular shaped proscenium stage for this crowd-pleaser, I prefer to use two round stages to draw attention to each musician. One benefit of round stages is that people can walk around them or be seated around them – although, of course, that is also a potential challenge for the performer, who must to remember to keep turning to face all sections of the audience.

The location, size, and height of the stage inevitably affects the impression, the visual dynamics, and the impact. If a speaker or a performer is on a 24" high platform in a small room, he or she will come across as a preacher "looking down" at the audience. This may not be the effect you want, especially if the speaker is talking about team building or working together.

Make sure your stage picture complements the speaker's message and the theme of the meeting.

Set design is critical, because it establishes

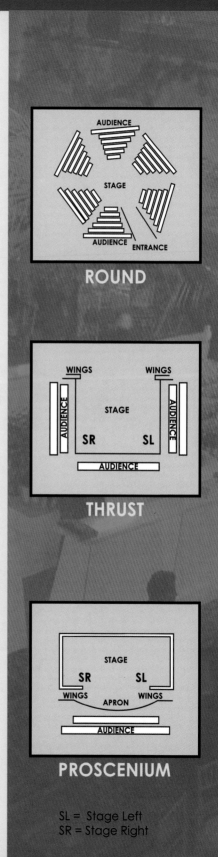

ROUND

THRUST

PROSCENIUM

SL = Stage Left
SR = Stage Right

A friend of mine, an audio-visual production professional Russ Ebersole, once designed and built drapes for a ballroom in a prestigious hotel in New York City. Working in this unique space, Russ realized that the stark black curtain he had "inherited" was hard on the attendees' eyes and was throwing off the room's balance. He chose to use gold draping instead, which blended into the existing décor and made the screen wall on which the images would be projected "seamless" to

the viewer. Draping is one of the great staging secrets of experienced event planners. www.drapekings.com.

Images: King Cole

the visual and spatial first impression participants receive upon entering a room. For events, I advise my students that if they are in a big space with a limited budget, the stage should focus on *one* specific area; on the other hand, if they are in a small space with an ample budget, they should focus on *multiple* details.

There is no one hard-and-fast rule that will result in successful staging. The placement of stage elements must be based on what has to be included in the production. Podiums, for instance, may have to be moved or removed to accommodate the next item on the agenda.

I once set the stage for an executive level Human Resources meeting featuring a session on diversity. For this I "shopped" in the hotel and found five chairs of strikingly different shapes and sizes ranging from a bar stool to a boardroom chair for the panelists. This delivered quite a strong visual effect when the attendees walked in. At another time, for a non-profit children's gala, I designed the name of the foundation in children's blocks and suspended them on the stage – another simple and effective visual statement.

Think of the stage as a component of a design palette offering countless choices and combinations. For instance, a portable stage can be carpeted in different colors; similarly, the draping along the edge of the stage can be made from a variety of materials that complement the color scheme on stage.

Another important element of staging is projection. The options must be considered in tandem with all the questions that accompany effective audiovisual production. How big is the room? Is the staging part of a meeting or a large event? What content must be projected? Is front or rear projection being used? Is the event being webcast or videotaped? Is there a built-in projection room? What lighting is available, and how will it affect the audience's ability to see and read from the screen? The same projectors used in a boardroom cannot be used in a ballroom.

What we choose to project the message on is another important consideration. There are many innovative and creative possibilities when it comes to screens and projected surfaces, but here again, you must be careful to match the medium with the message, and to take into account all the environmental factors (such as whether the projection will take place inside or outside). We can project the message on many innovative surfaces: fabric panels, spandex, water walls, or buildings. Obviously, a serious presentation about impending budget cutbacks will not have the desired effect if it is delivered on a white, suspended star-shaped spandex panel.

Consider the options; take things like setup time and room dimensions into account, and use the screen that does the best job of supporting your story. Be dramatic.

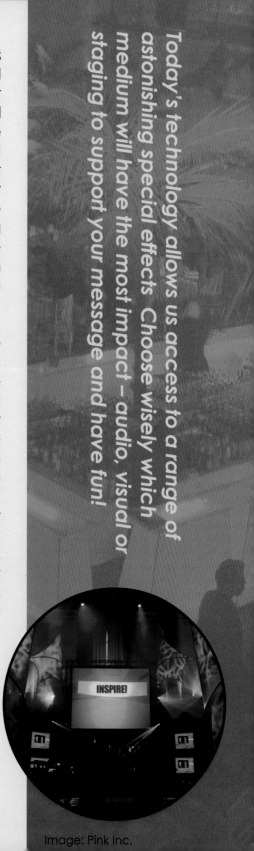

Today's technology allows us access to a range of astonishing special effects. Choose wisely which medium will have the most impact – audio, visual or staging to support your message and have fun!

Image: Pink Inc.

THE CONNECTIVITY FACTOR

Today's amazing advances in technology will continue to affect all technical production options — and, by extension, virtually all aspects of meetings and events by doing a better job of connecting event designers with marketing data, logistics information and stakeholders needs. The more robust the program, the better Return On Event.

Because of the astonishing advances in technology at our disposal, I believe the future of meetings and events is one in which people connect in ways that once seemed impossible. Integrated products like MetaMeetings® by MAPDigital will continue to give meeting and event professionals more and better choices, and the next generation of multi-platform programs will offer a fully integrated user experience — live, on demand, anywhere, at anytime. These advances – and others even we can't imagine — will continue to affect our planning and our physical set- ups ... and give us more choices that support the creative use of space, audiovisual and staging. Fasten your seat belts! With every new technological advance comes the opportunity to do a better job of conveying, enhancing, and reinforcing the message.

Multi-platform programs offer a fully integrated user experience — live, on demand, anywhere, at anytime.

THE PLAN'S THE THING!

Event designers and producers who know their business will confirm that the most effective, powerful, and memorable events are, ultimately, shows. That means you, as an event professional, are in show business. You have the responsibility to stage a good show, which means you have the responsibility to schedule the time necessary to plan a good show. By the same token, you can't escape the responsibility for designing a good show because you don't have the same level of technical knowledge as the experts in such fields as carpentry, lighting, and sound. You must work with the experts in the field, ahead of time, to create and execute a compelling plan for your production.

THIS SPACE FOR
DOODLING & NOTES

"When you come into the theater, you have to be willing to say, "We're all here to undergo a communion."
— David Mamet

Lighting Design: Cue Sheet

This lists the lighting cues as recorded at the opening of the 2001 production at Cumbernauld Theatre on 8 February and re-interpreted by the Company Stage Manager to relight the show while on tour. It should be read in combination with the other materials relating to the lighting design, as the cryptic terms such as 'TABLE 1' refer to particular lights or groups of lights that are identified in the lighting plans and the list of the 'Specials and General States'.

The words in bold at the beginning of each cue indicate the point at which the cue was given and the lights changed. So a cue point 'END OF SCENE 3' would indicate the point at which the lighting for Scene 4 would be cued.

Abbreviations used

S = seconds (eg 5S = a change taking 5 seconds)
DS/US/MID DS = Downstage/Upstage/Mid-downstage etc
HL = house lights
FOH = Front of House
↗↗↗ = three lights from downstage right/front of house right
↙ = one light from upstage left
↗↖ = two lights, one from each side and downstage
←← = two lights from the side (stage left)
↓↓↓↓ = four top lights or back lights from roughly centre stage
Other arrows have similar meanings

1. ↖↖↖ GEN STRAW / WARM GENERAL AREA COVER SIX AREAS IN
   ↖↖↖ LEE 764 SUN COLOUR STRAW. FRESNELS OR WIDE SOFT PROFILE.

2. ↗↗↗ GEN O/W GENERAL AREA COVER SAME AS ABOVE FROM
   ↗↗↗ OTHER DIRECTION. OPEN WHITE. FRESNELS OR WIDE SOFT PROFILE.

3. ↓↓↓ WARM BACK GENERAL BACKLIGHT IN SIX AREAS. LEE 009
   ↓↓↓ FRESNELS OR FLOODS AT A PINCH.

4. ↓↓ BLUE BACK GENERAL BACKLIGHT IN FOUR AREAS. LEE 161,
   ↓↓ FRESNELS OR FLOODS AT A PINCH.

5. ↗↗ FOH AMBER FILL GENERAL PROFILE WASH IN FOUR AREAS
   ↗↗ SHALLOW ANGLE (LONG WAY AWAY) PROFILES. LEE 134.

6. ↑↑ BLUE GENERAL FRESNEL WASH FROM STRAIGHT ON IN
   ↑↑ FOUR AREAS. LEE 201.

7. ←← MOON FILL (ALSO IN "ALL BLUES") GENERAL TOP SIDE FRESNEL
   COVER OVER WHOLE STAGE IN TWO LARGE OVERLAPPING AREAS. LEE 196.

8. AMB ↙ HILL SINGLE FRESNEL FROM BACK OF HILL FAIRLY WIDE FO-
   CUSED. LEE 134. FAIRLY VITAL.

9. Y ↗ HILL SINGLE PROFILE SHALLOW ANGLE FLAT ON TO HILL TO LIFT THE YELLOW CORN. LEE 765. MUST BE WIDE ENOUGH TO COVER WHOLE HILL.

10. WARM ↗ HILL TWO 500W SMALL FRESNELS OR PROFILES ONE FOR TOP OF HILL, ONE FOR LOWER BIT, OVERLAP A LOT, PAIRED. HELP TO TAKE THE GENERAL UP THE HILL. LEE 764.

11. COLD ↗ HILL SAME AS ABOVE IN LEE 201.

12. SKY COVER THE SKY IN LEE 119 DARK BLUE / 196 LIGHTER BLUE / BIT OF RED, BIT OF AMBER AND MIX THE RESULT.

13. TABLE 1 TWO WIDE FRESNELS LIGHTING DSC AREA IN LEE 009 TO GIVE A KITCHEN AREA. BETTER TOO WIDE THAN NOT ENOUGH.

14. TABLE 5 SINGLE WIDE FRESNEL IN O/W TO LIGHT USR CORNER BUT FAR ENOUGH DOWN TO WORK FOR THE SOLICITORS AND CONSCRIPTION. (there is no table 2,3,4)

15. →← PAIR OF PROFILES LIGHTING A STRIP FAR DS ABOUT TWO METERS WIDE AND COVERING THE FULL WIDTH IN O/W.

16. WEDDING PAIR OF PAR CANS MED OR WIDE DEPENDING ON VENUE SIZE FROM THE TOP SIDES JUST UNDER HALF WAY BACK FOR CROSS LIGHT IN LEE 09.

17. MOON PAR SPECIAL PAR CAN MED OR WIDE DEPENDING ON VENUE SIZE, TINY BIT UP FROM DSC IN LEE 201 FOR KORA'S SONGS.

18. DSC SPECIAL PROFILE SOFT FOCUS DSC IN O/W FOR FILL AND KORA'S SONGS. THIS HELPS TO FILL THE MIDDLE OF →←

19. DSL SPECIAL QUITE WIDE AREA PROFILE IN 09 SOFT FOCUS TO CATCH SOMEONE STANDING DSC. BEWARE LIGHTING FEET BUT NOT HEADS.

20. BIRTH TWO W⋯ DO) OR FRESNE⋯ FRONT. IF ONLY ⋯

21. SIDE → PINK⋯ TOP AND ONE LO⋯ IT THE TOP ONE. ⋯

22. SIDE → BLUE⋯

23. BIRDIES FRONT⋯

24. FIRE FLOODS A⋯ FIRE THING. ANYT⋯

25. LIGHTNING AN⋯ ANGLE. LIGHT BLU⋯

"I regard the theatre as the greatest of all art forms, the most immediate way in which a human being can share with another the sense of what it is to be a human being." — Oscar Wilde

PART 4:
PAINTING THE PICTURE

Blending the Colors of Your Palette

If we cannot have fun and connect as people, we lose the chance to convey our message. If we miss that opportunity, we also lose a little of our humanity, our spirit, and our reason for committing to any cause in the first place. We miss out on some of the things our ancestors knew were important when they began the human journey with ritual celebrations that defined and consolidated the first communities.

We now know that the era of one-size-fits-all "theme parties," which drove business gatherings from the mid-1970s into the early 1990s, will never be repeated. Society has shifted to a different paradigm. These seemingly frivolous gatherings were catalysts to forging life-long relationships that this industry is built on, all done in the spirit of serious fun. They appealed to the boomer generation. There wasn't one moment that the people who attended these events forgot they were working; that their dance partner could be their client, or employee the next day.

Artist: Kathy McGilvray, NYC

THIS SPACE FOR
DOODLING & NOTES

*IN THE END, THERE
ARE NO WALLS
IN A WELL
DESIGNED EVENT!*

Now, as meetings and events continue to evolve and prove their value as communication vehicles and as the "return on event" to the organization becomes an object of greater concern, there is a responsibility for planners, designers, and producers to move beyond one-dimensional themes. To do that, they must acknowledge the importance of:

a) Determining the strategic intent of the story to be told
b) Branding the experience
c) Integrating attendee involvement,
d) Involving social media: and
e) Designing based on emotional responses from human beings

If you've come this far, you've seen many examples of the planning, the thought process it takes to design and produce off the paramount event. What's left? Creativity!

Creativity is a funny animal. You can't pick a time to be creative or set aside specific hours in the day to generate ideas. You can't easily define creativity until you see it, but you recognize it when it's there. The more people you allow to participate, the better your chances are of coming up with something good – hence the popularity of group "brainstorming" sessions.

This section is meant to initiate that kind of session. It's designed to share ideas that can inspire you when you are planning and producing a completely integrated event.

I can't tell you where or how the ideas in this section evolved, but along the way they helped deliver a message, find a solution, liven up a few hours in somebody's day, or get the kind of chuckle or smile that turns into inspiration, motivation and eventually a successful business result and relationship.

My hope is that, by reviewing a variety of ideas relating to specific events that have worked for me over the years, a light bulb will glow somewherein your mind and ignite an idea for your own event. Use the ideas you and your team generate within the framework of the objectives, the context, and the level of the event you are planning.

Involvement is everything. Years ago, I would pass a nickel around my classroom and ask my students to remember Dianne's "Five Sense Rule" – the rule that every choice we make as designers must engage one or more of the senses – and thus engage the participant. Now I call it the "Sixth Sense Rule" – to encompass that all-important "sense" that comes into play with the participant's willing suspension of disbelief. Involvements through that sixth sense, the sense that takes down both physical walls and the barriers between people, is what makes all involvement – both physical and virtual – happen.

Be influenced by the following, but don't try to fol the idea needed to spark the BIG reaction and create the memory in the name of serious fun.

> With any interactive event, there will always be attendees who want to sit and converse. Establish a 'quiet' area to allow this interaction.

Image: Props for Today

Inspiration for the name of your "theme idea" could include:

- Using current events such as movies, songs, television shows

- Using (getting inspiration from) historic plays and playwrights

- Playing with words (almost the same things as puns)

- Playing with puns

- Using car and vehicle names

- Using something personal to the specific host or audience

- Using current popular slang expressions (in good taste)

- Accenting the destination, location, and venue

- Using history, museums, famous landmarks, and attractions

- Famous people

- Inserting your company or family name into popular titles of shows

- Using the colors associated with the event

- Video games

- Researching your theme to find new ideas that spark your imagination

Choose what you need and leave the rest. And, most of all, **enjoy the process!**

THE NAME GAME

The name or *theme* of an event is often (but not always) one and the same.

The theme name is the first opportunity to entice your guests and create a buzz that will grasp their attention. A clever name given to a common theme will provoke curiosity about the event and be provocative – it is part of marketing for the event. The chosen name will often imply details that relate to the super objective and vision. The relationship of the name to the graphic and/or logo will be remembered and identify the experience. How you translate the theme name into a theme style is the basis for what follows.

Finding the perfect name to match your theme is part of the craft of event design.

Use these simple and easy sample theme names and ideas as brainstorm exercises. Remember – the event delivers the message through the story that is being told in progression.

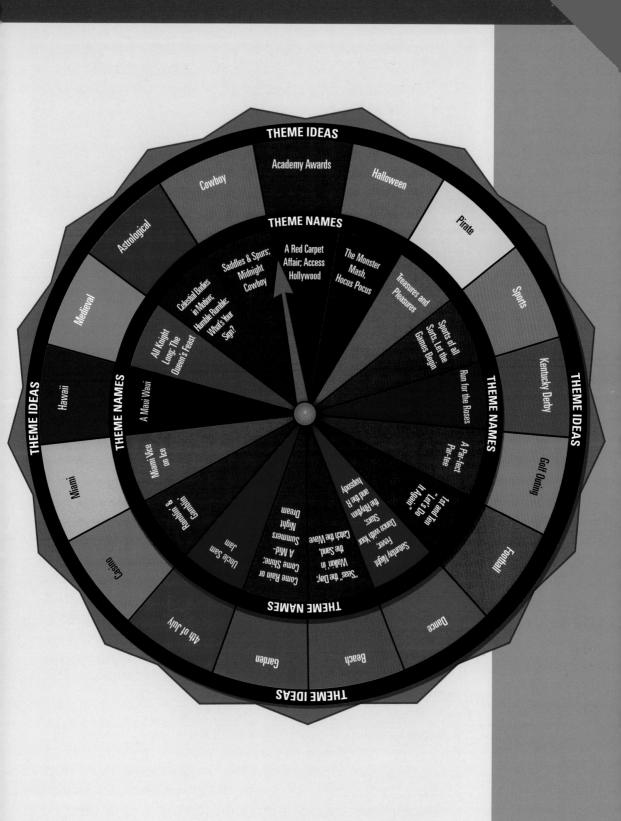

THEME IDEAS

Academy Awards

Cowboy

Halloween

Astrological

Pirate

Medieval

THEME NAMES

Saddles & Spurs;
Midnight
Cowboy

A Red Carpet
Affair; Access
Hollywood

The Monster
Mash,
Hocus Pocus

Celestial Bodies
in Motion;
Humble Humble;
What's Your
Sign?

All Knight
Long; The
Queen's Feast

Treasures and
Pleasures

Sports

Sports of all
Sorts; Let the
Games Begin

Hawaii

A Maui Waui

Run for the Roses

Kentucky Derby

THEME IDEAS

THEME NAMES

THEME NAMES

THEME IDEAS

Miami 'Vice
on Ice

A Par-fect
Par-tee

Golf Outing

Miami

Ramblin' &
Gamblin'

"Let's Do
1st and Ten
It Again"

Uncle Sam
Jam

"Seas" the Day;
Walkin' in
the Sand;
Catch the Wave

Saturday Night
Fever;
Dance with Your
Stars;
the Rhythm
and the R
hapsody

Come Rain or
Come Shine; A
Mid-
Summers
Night
Dream

Football

Casino

4th of July

Garden

Beach

Dance

THEME NAMES

THEME IDEAS

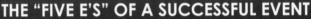

THE "FIVE E'S" OF A SUCCESSFUL EVENT

The Five E's process will help you to combine all the elements and colors of your event so you can explain and present to stakeholders. They coincide with the Five E's. You can begin the process of visualizing the experience and connecting the moments by realizing that the event is a fluid entity with (technically) no beginning or end.

PROGRESSION THROUGH THE "FIVE E'S"

Any event needs your attention in five critical "E" areas. Skipping any one of these "E" issues loses the impact to paint a picture and tell the story. Consult the list below closely before you start planning your event.

Pre/Before

1. Envision. This is where the theme is cultivated. This concept should be reflected in the name of the event. You should be able to briefly explain the content, visual dynamics, kinetic engineering of the event – timing, tempo and flow. Everything that the prospective participant sees, hears, and experiences about the event before actually encountering it in physical space falls under this first "E." These efforts are to entice and generate interest – they are the foundation of marketing and relate to the objectives and goals.

Live/During

2. Entrance Upon arrival, attendees leave their world and enter one of suspended reality. The entrance is the guests' first spatial experience of the event and has to immediately engage and invoke an emotional attachment. The theme should be instantly recognized, creating further anticipation as the event unfolds.

3. Experience: The event's experience is "all in the details," and every detail has to dovetail with the theme, further immersing the participant. This is the execution that includes production elements, food, beverages, music, entertainment, mood enhancers. This is where design, styling, and production meet to connect the 'story' and sustain attendee involvement and interest.

The theme should be instantly recognized, creating further anticipation as the event unfolds.

4. Exit: The exit is your guest's final impression of the event. The exit should maintain the integrity of the theme, leave a branding message, express your gratitude and reinforce the participant's reason for attending.

Post/After

5. Extend: This is two-fold. It is the post-event marketing that involves more than evaluations, thank yous, and phone calls. It allows for the development and content of the next live experience through the data collected in the pre-stage, the registration process. Secondly, it is the marketing connection to the attendees that grows and generates brand loyalty, keeping attendees linked through social media and technology. Post event follow up also allows for further discussion and development of issues and topics that were left unresolved.

STORYBOARD IT!

Creativity and creative thinking is an aerobic exercise for the brain. Rip out pictures, make notes, save samples in a file called "Inspiration" for reference. It might be a designer pen, a room look, furniture, or a custom decal for the dinner plate.

An integral part of designing and planning is 'seeing' the vision; living it and gathering concepts, building parts and materials, that will make it happen.

The best ideas and concepts have been written on scraps of paper and on paper napkins. Draw the story to be told to help conceptualize the experience and 'see' it. When you visualize it clearly, the design and planning process will flow naturally. How will you use the palette of choices – décor, food and beverage, floral, linen, music, entertainment – the visual dynamic—kinetic engineering – risk management.

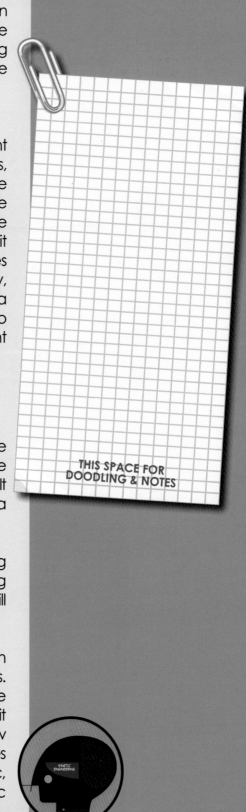

THIS SPACE FOR
DOODLING & NOTES

WHAT COLOR IS YOUR EVENT? WORKSHEET:
Dianne Budion Devitt

Objective: _____

Goals: _____
_____
_____

Theme: (objective + goals): _____

The Name Game (Give your theme a name): _____
_____

Paint the Picture: (the 5 E's)
1. Event Theme Name/Envision: _____

Explain: _____
_____
_____
_____

2. Entrance: _____
_____
_____
_____

3. Experience: _____
_____
_____
_____

4. Exit: _____
_____
_____

5. Extend: _____
_____
_____

STORYBOARD WORKSHEET

Event Theme/Name
_____
_____
_____
_____
_____
_____
_____
_____

[ ]

Entrance
_____
_____
_____

[ ]

Experience
_____
_____
_____

[ ]

Experience
_____
_____
_____

[ ]

Exit
_____
_____
_____

[ ]

Extend
_____
_____
_____

DYNAMICS OF CREATING A STORYBOARD

STORYBOARD WORKSHEET

Event Theme/Name

CLIENT APPRECIATION EVENT.
JOURNEY TO SUCCESS.
LONG ROAD TRAVELED.
TRANSFORMATION
OF SURROUNDINGS.

KASHMIR!

Entrance

COLORFUL DRAPERY, COVERED
TABLES, RED CARPET!

BLUE & RED DRAPES! CALL CLOTH COMPANY.

CALL TALENT AGENCY

CALL AUDIO PRODUCTION COMPANY

Experience

BLUE & RED LIGHTING, BACK-
LIT CAMEL. BELLY DANCERS!

Experience

LIVE MUSIC. BAND SHOULD
WEAR FEZ HATS. FORTUNE
TELLERS.

ART DIRECTOR NEEDS TO DESIGN MATERIALS

Exit

LIGHT & IMAGE PROJECTION
ON ALL WALLS. COSTUMES!

Extended

COLLATERAL EVALUATIONS.
E-MARKETING. FEZ HATS!

PROJECTION LIGHTING COMPANY

STORYBOARD WORKSHEET

Event Theme/Name

CLIENT APPRECIATION EVENT.
JOURNEY TO SUCCESS.
LONG ROAD TRAVELED.
TRANSFORMATION
OF SURROUNDINGS.

KASHMIR!
SUCCESS!!!

Entrance

COLORFUL DRAPERY, COVERED
TABLES, RED CARPET!

Experience

Experience

BLUE & RED LIGHTING, BACK-
LIT CAMEL. BELLY DANCERS!

LIVE MUSIC. BAND SHOULD
WEAR FEZ HATS. FORTUNE
TELLERS.

Exit

Extended

LIGHT & IMAGE PROJECTION
ON ALL WALLS. COSTUMES!

COLLATERAL EVALUATIONS.
E-MARKETING. FEZ HATS!

"Rock On!"

The description below is a sample of identifying a theme, relating to the host's objectives and goals, identifying the audience and creating an experience based on their profile. "Five E's" Event Example: "Rock On!" (video game)

Objective: To create an awards and incentive party for a team of sales people in their late 20s to 30's.

Goals:
- Celebrate achievements in a positive, open atmosphere
- Motivate the finest achievers (top sellers).
- Provide interactive activity

Envision:
Event Theme: Rock On!
Event Name: Guitar Heroes … Party like a Rock Star!

Using the Guitar Hero game and scoring rules, guests will "rock on" in a lively party atmosphere built around an interactive contest activity that identifies winners as "Heroes" and "Rock Stars." This event is designed to appeal to the competitive nature of certain groups, and promotes interaction and teambuilding. This concept can be done(executed) as the stand alone entertainment segment of an event.

Entrance: Red carpet walkway or a walkway shaped like guitars or music notes; walk through, under or in between an entrance that boasts oversized rock stars' photographs, guitars, or posters. Fans and paparazzi line the red carpet while a loop of current and classic rock music is played.

Experience: "Backstage Passes" are used for nametags. Use a popular DJ or a local Radio Host. Guests enter a room that has comfortable seating areas, food service stations,

Choose what you need and leave the rest.

a bar, a stage that is designed to be easily accessible to the "Hero" contestants, plus a fake radio station set that will house the DJ/Live Radio Broadcast and announcer for the evening. The stage will have the Guitar Hero set to include the Guitar Hero equipment, a full-size screen on the stage with life-size cutouts of famous male and female rock stars. All cut outs have the face missing for photo opportunities for the guests. Video screens provide MTV & VH1 footage of current and past rock videos. Food stations include traditional American cuisine with an upscale preparation. The bar is full service, and boasts specialty drinks that are named for famous rock stars. The décor includes guitars, vinyl records, neon signs, a single or several table top juke boxes, and star cut outs and projections. The Guitar Hero game begins with an announcement from the DJ and the event begins.

Exit: At the conclusion is the announcement of the "Heroes" and winners. Guests exit as they arrived and are greeted by staff who offer their congratulations and an assortment of gifts that could range from donations in their name to "Save the Music" ***http://www.vh1savethemusic.com/donation***, "Rock and Wrap it Up! "***http://win4hunger.org/*** or, budget allowing, I-Pods, headsets, and other such items that are often placed in the Grammy's giveaway bags.

Extend: Sent their own customized CD's from the event with a message from the host, receive emails from the selected charities or causes, have their photos on line, download their 'performances' for non-attendees to see, start a twitter group of "Your Guitar Heroes." Rank the 'performances' against actual work performance in the future.

THIS SPACE FOR
DOODLING & NOTES

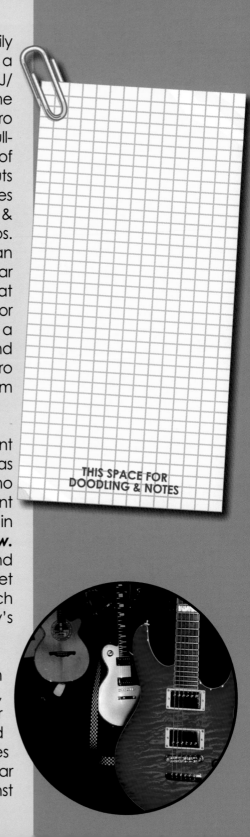

More Brainstorming Ideas!

- Have concert ticket invitations delivered prior to the event.
- Add the "Rock Band" element to the Guitar Hero gaming equipment.
- Provide Rock Trivia booklets, Rock Star Jumbles and such games at the guests' tables or seating areas.
- Engage guests who are not playing in the Guitar Hero contest by a Name that Tune contest or a Karaoke contest.
- Have a CD recording booth on site for guests to make their own vocal recording.
- Set up a dress-up area that includes wigs, jewelry, sunglasses & studded jackets for accessorizing..
- Have pin ball machines or "Dance Dance Revolution" games in a designated game area.
- Have a videographer on hand to project live interviews and guests interactions on video monitors set to rock music.
- Have a tattoo artist on hand.
- Give the guests some bling!
- Have a camera crew and interviewer asking their opinions of this party and show the interview simultaneously on exit video monitors.
- Create a branded T-Shirt
- Give away a pair of drumsticks engraved with the company name.
- Or, just splurge and give them a Guitar Hero game!

"The theme allows for an event that is fun and relevant to this young company. The name achieves the clients objective in that it is inherently motivational and describes a party for winners as "Heroes" & "Rock Stars." It allows for interactive activity and will reinforce a subtle competitive and necessary element to the success of their performance." Says who? Should the quotation marks be there?

Event Sample #2

Envision:
Event Theme: Theatre
Event Name: Give Our Regards to Broadway/Broadway Bound

This event can work for almost any group who is celebrating, recognizing, awarding or just need a familiar theme. It can be applied to featuring a new product as the 'show' and can be produced minimally with maximum effects.

Explanation: Bring the excitement of the theatre to your guests. This celebration in song and dance is an experience that re-creates the thrill of seeing a live Broadway show. Give Our Regards to Broadway will create a theatrical atmosphere with options from comedy to drama. It's an educational opportunity to focus on different playwrights and their works.

Entrance:
- Video monitors run show-stopping musical performances from Broadway shows.
- Mock theatre entrance or back-stage look(atmosphere enhanced) with ladders, ropes, equipment, set pieces, make-up tables, and costume racks.
- The sale of raffle tickets for orchestra seats to a current running Broadway or local show.
- Accessorizing guests with feather boas, top hats, canes, wigs, tap shoes, Broadway show tune songbooks, and scripts.
- Display Broadway show posters and programs.
- Create a "cast list" poster set on a tripod, singling (which singles out) out prominent event or company individuals, contributors, and sponsors.
- Employ a tuxedoed staff (staff in formal tuxedoes), and or singing waiters and waitresses.
- Utilize red velvet ropes and a red carpet welcome path.
- Hire actors as paparazzi to take pictures that will become available to the guests as they exit.

THIS SPACE FOR
DOODLING & NOTES

Experience:
- Create a stage boasting a simple, glittering gold, silver or Theatre Row backdrop accented with tassel back draped velvet curtains. Use backdrops for scenes.
- Build authentic stage sets.
- Feature menu items named after Broadway shows or songs.
- Use old scripts or play books.
- Employ a lighting designer for state-of-the-art lighting effects.
- Hire actors and performers to sing and dance.
- Construct a simple stage area with a microphone and the use of Broadway Karaoke.
- Cocktail hour can include unique Broadway show named drinks.
- Awards for company employees or special guests can be given in the name of the "Tony".
- As the evening comes to an end, guests are instructed to sing along for the grand finale. Pick a song with words projected for all to see.
- Chance drawing Raffle for autographed poster from a top hit show

Exit:
- The master of ceremonies gives a parting speech saying that "each and everyone" is "one singular sensation," a song from "A Chorus Line" as a live chorus line of performers creates a kick-line towards the doors.
- Guests are handed newspapers with the "reviews" (a pre-written description of the event), which will also serve as an opportunity to distribute any company information.

Extend: (refer to description and apply use of this function for business)
* Introduce guests to different Broadway and Actors charities; keep informed of special ticket offers; conduct a silent auction online to raise funds that could include dinner with a Broadway performer.

More Ideas: You Do the Brainstorming!

Envision:
Event Theme: Beach (or any nature environment)
Event Name: Making Waves; _____

This experience is best applied when an escape to the freedom and carefree spirit a summer feeling brings is needed any time of year. Creating an open environment and encouraging interaction through an open environment promotes ease and comfort in networking and interacting.

This theme could work when there is tension or conflict among groups or when bringing people together from different locales. The connotation of outdoors and being in nature, frees us and can be an instant team builder.

Engage:

Entrance includes sounds of waves, sand, flip flops, palm trees, lifeguard on stand, boats, kites suspended, 'plane' with message, convertible car, beach balls on floor, primping stations, sunglasses, novelty glasses, visors or summer hats, flip flops given out.

Experience:

Real sand dance floor, colorful sun-umbrellas, beach towels and toys, sand toys, shells and starfish, volleyballs and net, backgammon boards with champion players, surfboards, fishing gear and nets, mermaids, dolphins, body builders, videos of old/new beach films/TV shows (with permission) be shown. A steel drum band, summer music, tropical drinks, summer food menu like barbecue, fried chicken and salads, a themed packed lunch, or a clambake dinner, dune buggy, chaise lounges, summer furniture.

Exit: Pass out a 'green' beach bag or information on how to save the whales, clean the ocean, dolphins, sea turtles, and dune erosion.

Extend: What options can involve the group in an environmental cause and keep your organization linked to its corporate social responsibility goals? Maintaining relationships and recruiting volunteers is a great way to forge future relationships.

Dianne Says:

"Use edible center-pieces: grapes and fruit placed among florals in the center of the table."

Envision

Event Theme: *The Renaissance*
Event Name: Eat, Drink, Be Merry/It's Good to be Queen/Reign for a Day.

This is more formal 'edutainment' as designing a period theme provides an opportunity for educating and linking historic accuracy. Using a 'feast' theme the setting urges participation in an open, ribald environment. Its character represents sharing and passing food, which is a subliminal team builder encouraging conversation as well as enjoyment. Its concept can be toned down to be more formal or built up to be more lively and bold.

Engage: "Town crier," suits of armor, jugglers, court jesters, knights and gypsies. Create a mystical medieval world where ravens, dragons and fairies play. The setting is a Gothic stone castle, a chateau, or even a tent or a facade to replicate one. Use a 'draw bridge' crossing or cobblestone pathway done through lighting.

Experience:

Decorate with stained glass, gargoyles, dragons, trumpets, banners, coats of arms, garlands, swords, daggers, tapestries, fresh and dried flowers in rich dark colors, candelabras, large rugs on the floor, lit torches and parchment scrolls with lettering done in calligraphy. (Refer to artists of the period for added inspiration!)

Huge prop candelabras and mock (lit) chandeliers will give the effect of a hallway full of candles. Traditional food includes turkey legs with big loaves of bread, or a more elaborate feast including game meats including venison and goose that were common along with cheeses, nuts, berries, tarts and custards. Drinks could include ale, beer, wine, and fruit juices served in big wooden goblets or pewter mugs. One long wooden table or a series of long wooden tables could be draped in heavy velvet fabrics with tapestry runners. Use pewter plates and cups. Entertain with mimes, magicians, belly dancers, astrologers, a jousting troupe, country dancers, and minstrel music. Costume the staff in a variety of styles that represent wenches, bar maids, virgin maidens, lords, merchants, knights, kings and queens. Include a glossary of "Olde English" terms for the guests amusement. Have chess game tables available. Utilize a family shield to display your company or event logo. Have a falconry demonstration. Play human chess on a black and white dance floor.

Exit: Distribute muslin gift bags with journals and quill pens so participants remember this most interesting experience; give out a copy of one of Shakespeare's plays; donate to a local theater group.

Extend: Marketing involvement could include charity work, specifically donating turkeys around Thanksgiving. Use period for any product compatibility?? Develop relationship with chess associations and engage guests in on-line contest to attend tournament.

THIS SPACE FOR
DOODLING & NOTES

Envision:

Event Theme: *Black and White (color)*

Event Name: Ebony and Ivory

A Black and White party (or any color theme) is cost-effective simple way to custom design almost any event. Involve your guests by encouraging a black and white dress code and let dress become movable decor.

Entrance: Guests arrive to the venue on a black or white rolled out carpet, customized floor decals, lighting effects, loose balloons (careful), a snow machine (caution for slippery floor). Spandex walls, columns, arches, wind chimes, lighting effects, and white flower arrangements introduce the simple elegance that will define this event.

Experience: The floor is white and black. The walls are white. Projections change color. More snow. The room's design is a white canvas just waiting for your personal touch. The entrance features white pillars and balustrades, life-like Dalmatian ceramics, white doves in antique birdcages with architectural lighting. White and black fabric including zebra stripes, lattice and cool lighting define the space. Ice carvings, white linens, crystal and china. A black-tie or funky white t-shirt/black pants wait staff. Customize your bar choices and name your drinks after famous film noir stars or play black and white silent films. Don't forget Truman Capote who is known for creating the most celebrated black and white party in Hollywood – or keep a nightclub atmosphere with two white baby grand pianos in a dueling piano performance both sitting on individual round stages. Display black and white photographs and project black and white videos and films for added interest. Utilize designs that include piano keys and chessboards at buffet tables and on floors. Employ pianists at black and white pianos or harpists for entertainment. Accessorize your guests with masks, fans, feather boas, and top hats.

Exit: Donations to local artists, musicians and animal groups. A special gift could include the 'roll-up' piano keyboards with sheet music for beginners.

Envision: ?_____

Theme: *Speakeasy*
Event Name: Prohibition: What's the Password?

Explanation: The Gatsby Era was a time of drama and energy. The well-heeled sought excitement in back alley speakeasies where bathtub gin flowed with abandon and the music was all Jazz. It was an age of innocence, prosperity and optimism. This topic could be appropriate for new groups to meet each other or as a new product launch.

Entrance: Guests enter through a classic speakeasy door with a sliding peephole. A secret password allows them into the "Roaring Twenties" speakeasy bar. There, bartenders with garters on their sleeves serve a variety of cocktails including "Moonshine." Flappers with long pearl necklaces and rolled down stockings sip champagne as they sit on the bar holding cigarettes from long cigarette holders. Cocktails are served in teacups in true Prohibition style. Women are given sequined headbands, boas, and pearl necklaces. Men receive bowties, gloves, and gangster hats.

There are signed pictures on the walls from Al Capone, Bugsy Siegel and Babe Ruth. A piano player plays ragtime music.

Experience: The Speakeasy is suddenly raided by characters dressed as Keystone Cops or your own local police. Rotating mirrored balls are hung from the ceiling. Zebra-skin accented fabrics, sunburst shapes, and zigzagged patterns are visual highlights. Suddenly linens appear and cover the room to look like a place of worship. The maître'd quickly puts on a robe and becomes a preacher. Guests are seated for dinner and a tuxedoed staff wearing white gloves

THIS SPACE FOR
DOODLING & NOTES

serves an elegant dinner fare. Guests are then treated to parlor tricks, séances, fortune telling and perhaps even casino gaming all while a Big Band, backed by a city skyline and clad in zoot suits perform. A Master of Ceremonies introduces featured singers who could be Al Jolson and Louis Armstrong impersonators. The music continues throughout the evening while dance instructors lead guests in dancing the Charleston and the Shimmy. Could also be interpreted into a poker fest.

Exit: Guests receive a sealed envelope with a donation form, old black and white postcards, and a DVD of Bonnie and Clyde.

Extend: Use the Prohibition theme as a marketing concept that could be designed for a 'secret' group although it's the public. Social media and on-line participation could extend the concept and build these private experiences for your select target audience to meet either on line through Twitter groups or in person – all using the password that reinforces the brand.

Brainstorming the Event: An Example

Suppose you wanted to build your event around the idea of England. How many ideas could you come up with for each of the Five E's?

Envision

This event could acknowledge the grand traditions, history, and legends of England. It could be interactive, informal, and festive, or formal and serene.Entrance: Cobblestone streets; flower girls with carts; Covent Garden; double-decker buses; crisply dressed Bobbies; red telephone booths; backdrops with images of sites including the London Bridge, Big Ben, the Tower of London, Buckingham Palace, Westminster Abbey, Leicester Square, Piccadilly Square, the West End, or Oxford.

Experience: Vignettes of "Neverland" where Peter Pan and his boys are engaged in a duel with Captain Hook ; "The Casino" where James Bond is playing Baccarat against his archrivals from Specter, (Martinis, shaken not stirred are on hand); "Hogwarts Academy for Wizards", where Harry Potter is demonstrating his magic skills; "Mad Hatters Tea Party" where Alice and company are serving cakes and teas; and finally the Bard himself, William Shakespeare. The center of this space is reserved for merriment and revelry in an Old English Pub setting. Wait staff appears dressed in characters that continue in the English Fantasy style. Characters could include Austin Powers, Queen Victoria, Henry VIII, Sherlock Holmes, the Beatles, Tom Jones, and Monty Python to name a few. Guests may take photographs with the characters, visit their worlds, or just hang out in the pub partaking in games such as Dominoes, Cribbage, Billiards, Cricket (modified) or Darts, and of course eating anything from traditional fish and chips, Scotch eggs, roast beef and Yorkshire pudding, Bubble and Squeak, to mince pies and English crumpets. For entertainment guests are treated to traditional music hall variety show – or a modified version of a holiday Pantomime!

Exit: As guests leave they could be greeted by characters and given gifts such as Beefeater Teddy Bears, an assortment of Earl Grey teas, and other such British mementos. Alternatively, they can be informed that a donation was made to a British charity in lieu of gifts.

"When your event calls for a country-based theme, you can use entertainment as an educational opportunity to teach history, culture, and manners about the country in question."

More History-Based Ideas for Themes

1920s

- **History:** Presidents: Woodrow Wilson, Warren G. Harding, Calvin Coolidge and Herbert Hoover; Black Thursday; stock market crash; Henry Ford and mass production of the Model T. Ford; prohibition; Volstead Act; womens' suffrage; Charles Lindbergh's' first transatlantic flight.

- **Music:** The Jazz age: Al Jolson, Duke Ellington, Irving Berlin, Jelly Roll Morton, Bessie Smith, George Gershwin, Louis Armstrong, Bing Crosby. Chicago was hot and the Cotton Club in Harlem was packed nightly.

- **Radio:** The Golden Age of Radio; the Victrola aired variety shows, news, popular music and classical music, fictional stories and lectures. David Sarnoffs; NBC; William Paleys, CBS airs.

- **Movies:** Silent Movie Stars; Rudolph Valentino, Clara Bow, Rudy Valee, Charlie Chaplin, 1926, The Keystone Cops; first talking picture entitled the Jazz Singer.

- **Dance:** Dance Marathons: Charleston, Black Bottom & Shimmy, Fox Trot.

- **Art:** Bauhaus Harlem Renaissance, Surrealism 1920-1940. Example; Edward Hopper, Picasso, Miro.

- **Fashions:**
  Women: The Gibson girl & the Flapper: Bobbed hair, knee-high hemlines, long pearl necklaces, headbands, feathers, rolled down stockings, unbuckled galoshes, cloche hats, and furs.
  Men: The sacque suit, black bowler hats, top hat and tails, patent leather shoes and Oxford bags, knickers and sweaters.

- **Newsmakers:** Gangsters; speakeasy bars; moonshine, bathtub gin; Al Capone; Bugsy Siegel; the Great Gatsby; F. Scott Fitzgerald; first Miss America pageant; Babe Ruth; Jack Dempsey; Route 66; Harry Houdini magic; casinos and gambling; Winnie the Pooh and the First Oxford English Dictionary published; first Mickey Mouse Cartoon; sliced bread invented; 1st Academy awards.

1930s

- **Historical: Presidents:** Herbert Hoover and Franklin D. Roosevelt; economic despair; the Wagner Act and unionization; fireside chats; the New Deal.

- **Music:** Big Bands and the birth of Swing, Guy Lombardo, Louis Armstrong, Billy Holiday, Fats Waller, The Harlem Renaissance, Kate Smith sings "God Bless America", Duke Ellington.

- **Radio:** Reaches its peak; 1937, The Hindenburg disaster broadcast; Jack Benny, Amos and Andy, George Burns and Gracie Allen; Abbott & Costello "Who's on first"; Roosevelt's fireside chats; H.G.Well's War of the Worlds.

- **Film:** Hollywood's Golden Age: Gone with the Wind, The Grapes of Wrath, The Keystone Cops, The Little Rascals, The Wizard of Oz; Mickey Mouse and Betty Boop arrive; Clark Gable, Bette Davis, Greta Garbo, the Marx Brothers, Shirley Temple, Busby Berkley, Fred Astaire and Ginger Rogers; The Three Stooges.

- **Dance:** Lindy Hop, Jitterbug, swing, Lambeth Walk, the big apple, and Latin inspired Rumba and Conga.

- **Art:** American Gothic, Edward Hopper, Jackson Pollock.

- **Fashions:**
  Women: silk stockings, to the knee hemlines, turbans and brimmed hats. Permanent hair waves and use of make-up, furs. Skirts hemlines to the ankle.
  Men: Double-breasted suits and fedoras, the Palm Beach suit.

- **Newsmakers:** Depression Glass; Vaudeville; telegrams; soup kitchens; Tootsie Pops, Hershey Bars, Lifesavers, Neccos, Twinkies, Whitman's Samplers; comic books, yo-yos, die cast metal toys; hobos on railroads; the Volkswagen Beetle; Will Rogers, Amelia Earhart, Agatha Christie; NY World's Fair of 1939; Monopoly.

1940S

- **Historic:** Presidents: Franklin Roosevelt and Harry S. Truman; World War 11, the Japanese attack Pearl Harbor, Winston Churchill, D-Day; USO Canteen; War & Savings Bonds.

- **Music:** Swing; Big Bands, Glen Miller, Tommy Dorsey, Duke Ellington, Frank Sinatra, Bing Crosby, Dizzy Gillespie, Charlie Parker, Woody Herman, Ella Fitzgerald.

- **Radio:** Armed Forces Radio, soap operas, quiz shows, mystery stories, Bob Hope and the Pepsodent Show, Edgar Bergen and Charlie McCarthy, George Burns and Gracie Allen.

- **Film & Television: Films:** The Great MGM musicals, Alfred Hitchcock, Casablanca, Bonnie and Clyde, Citizen Kane, It's a Wonderful Life, Fantasia.
Television; Ted Mack Amateur hour, Texaco Star Theatre, Howdy Doody Show, Toast of the Town, The Philco Television Playhouse.

- **Dance:** Swing, Jitterbug, Lindy Hop

- **Art:** Abstract expressionism, 1945-1960: Jackson Pollack, Willem Kooning, Andrew Wyeth, and Alexander Calder.

- **Fashions:**
Women: Shoulder pads, tight sweaters, puffed sleeves, swing skirts for dancing, the bikini, hats, gloves, bobby socks and saddle shoes, shoulder length hair and rolled bangs and trousers.
Men: Dark suits, pipes hats, oversized coats, and the Zoot Suit.

- **Newsworthy:** Flags & Patriotism; fireworks; Betty Grable "the pin-up girl"; cigarette glamour girls; "Kilroy was here"; glider planes; frozen dinners; tupperware; slinkies; diners; Rosie the Riveter.

1950s

- **Historic:** Presidents: Harry S.Truman and Dwight D. Eisenhower; McCarthyism and paranoia; the Cold War; Sputnik launched; baby boomers.

- **Music:** Rock and Roll & Doo Wop; Patti Page, Fats Domino, Elvis Presley, Bill Haley, Johnny Cash, Charlie Parker, Miles Davis, Nat King Cole, Bill Haley and his Comets, Fabien, Little Richard, Bobbie Darin and Pat Boon, Tony Bennett, Peggy Lee, The Chipmunks.

- **Film and Television:**
  Films: Sunset Boulevard, Some Like It Hot, Singin' in the Rain, White Christmas, All about Eve.
  Teen Films: Rebel without a cause, A Summer Place; Surfing movies.
  Alien films: The Day the Earth Stood Still, The War of the Worlds.
  Television: The Ed Sullivan Show, The Lone Ranger, Adventures of Ozzie and Harriet, I love Lucy, Leave it to Beaver, Your Show of Shows with Sid Caesar, I Love Lucy, The Honeymooners, Leave it to Beaver, Lassie, Mickey Mouse Club, Captain Kangaroo, Betty Boop.

- **Dance:** The Limbo, the Jitterbug, the Stroll, the Twist, and the Hand Jive.

- **Art:** Andy Warhol,

- **Fashions:**
  Women: pony tails, penny loafers, bobby sox, saddle shoes and poodle skirts, slim suits and strapless evening gowns.
  Men: crew cuts, leather jackets, jeans, white T-shirts, letter sweaters.

- **Newsworthy:** The boomerang; bubblegum; car hops; soda fountains; cheeseburgers; Coke Bottle; hoola Hoops; frisbees; radio flyers; Mr. Potato Head; Candyland; Barbie doll; pez dispensers; Ouija boards and jukeboxes; Cadillac; 3-D glasses; Dean Martin and Jerry Lewis; Life Magazine; American Bandstand; Copacabana; the Rainbow Room; Frank Lloyd Wright; and Betty Boop.

1960s

- **Historic:** Presidents: Dwight D. Eisenhower, John F. Kennedy, Lyndon B. Johnson; Martin Luther King, I Have a Dream; Vietnam War, draft dodgers, anti-war protests; Civil Rights, Malcolm X; John Glenn orbits the moon; first Americans to walk on the moon.

- **Music:** Psychedelic, Folk and Pop Music, Motown, the Beatles, the Beach Boys, Led Zeppelin, Jefferson Airplane, Janis Joplin, Bob Dylan, The Four Seasons, The Supremes, Peter, Paul and Mary, The Beach Boys, Herman's Hermits, Herb Alpert and the Tijuana Brass, The Mamas and the Papas and Chubby Checker introduces the Twist!

- **Film and Television:**
  Films: Breakfast at Tiffanys, The Graduate, Doctor Zhivago, My Fair Lady, The Sound of Music, 2001 Space Odyssey, Easy Rider, Elvis movies, A Hard Days Night, **Television:** Laugh In, The Beverly Hillbillies, Star Trek, the Twilight Zone, Batman, Dick Van Dyke Show, The Andy Williams show.

- **Dance:** the Mashed Potato, the Swim, the Monkey, the Jerk, the Shimmy, the Twist, the Frug and the Pony.

- **Art:** Op, Pop and Minimal. Peter Max,

- **Fashions:**
  Women: Mod Fashions. Bell bottoms, tie-dyed shirts, go-go boots, mini skirts, love beads, fringe, Indian-inspired prints, A-Line dresses, baby doll dresses, bouffant hair styles, conservative Collegiate fashions, and Jackie Kennedy inspired fashions including the pill box hat.
  Men; Nehru jackets, paisley shirts, velvet trousers, long hair, bolder and brighter colors. Single breasted suits with slim tapered pants. And the afro.

- **Newsworthy:** Hippies; psychedelic drugs; flower power; sexual revolution; the Age of Aquarius; Woodstock; Haight-Ashbury; peace signs; surfing; transistor radios; buttons; Twiggy; Batman; Etch A Sketch®; colorforms; lava lamps; Gumby; beaded curtains.

Illustration: Anthony Parisi

1970s

- **Presidents:** Richard Nixon, Gerald Ford, Jimmy Carter. Vietnam War; Roe vs. Wade; Kent State massacre; Watergate; affirmative action; Earth Day.

- **Music:** Disco phenomenon; heavy metal; Punk Rock; Donna Summer, Gloria Gaynor, the Village People, the Bee Gees, and Rod Stewart, Billy Joel, Elton John, Bruce Springsteen, Aerosmith, Queen, Abba, The Carpenters, and on the radio; Wolfman Jack, Ricky Dees.

- **Film and Television:**
  Films: Love Story, Mash, Annie Hall, Apocalypse Now, Chinatown, A Clockwork Orange, the Exorcist, the Godfather, Saturday Night Fever, Rocky, Star Wars, Taxi Driver.
  Television: Laugh In, Saturday Night Live, All in the Family, The Brady Bunch, Sesame Street, Lavern and Shirley, Mary Tyler Moore show, Taxi, Carol Burnett Show, Sonny and Cher.

- **Dance:** Electric Boogaloo, Locking, the Hustle, Disco, the Bump, YMCA.

- **Art:** New Realism, Conceptual Art, and Performance Art

- **Fashions:**
  Women: Micro, mini, or maxi skirts, bellbottoms, patches, hot pants, earth shoes, clogs, and platform shoes, Annie Hall inspired men's wear for women, halter jumpsuits, granny dresses, granny glasses
  Men: Leisure suits, disco suits, trouser suits, jogging suits.

- **Newsworthy:** Mood rings; lava lamps; smiley faces; disco mirror balls; shag rugs; pet rocks; tattoos; Farah Fawcett hairstyles; skateboarding; spandex and Lycra®, men with long hair, pop art, Rubik's cube; 8-track tape players; string art and Patti Hearst; the waterbed.

1980s

- **Presidents:** Ronald Reagan & George Bush. Columbia; U.S. first reusable spacecraft is launched; Nancy Reagan "Just Say No"; Aids crisis; John Lennon's assassination; first test tube baby.

- **Music:** MTV, new wave, punk, hip-hop & rap. Michael Jackson, Blondie, Stevie Nicks, Styx, Neil Diamond, Kool and the Gang, Herbie Hancock, Videos: Thriller, Beat It, Billy Jean, Michael Jackson, Addicted to Love, Robert Palmer.

- **Film and Television:**
  Films: Arthur, Stephen Spielberg movies ie: E.T. Tootsie, The Big Chill
  Television: Roseanne, Cheers, The Wonder Years, The Golden Girls, Cosby Show, Oprah, 60 minutes, Dallas

- **Dance:** slam dancing, Lambada, breakdancing, the moonwalk, poppin' & lockin', Running Man, and Electric Boogie.

- **Art:** Neo Expressionism, Computer and Postmodern Classicism.

- **Fashions:**
  Women: Madonna-inspired fashions, Ann Klein, Donna Karan and Princess Diana.
  Men: Influenced by Calvin Klein, Michael Jackson and power dressing Yuppies.

- **Newsworthy:** Smurf; E.T; Paraphernalia; Nintendo; Pac Man; Game Boy; valley girls; Michael Jackson's glove; Jane Fonda workout videos; Richard Simmons; Trivial Pursuit; Cabbage Patch dolls; Teenage Mutant Ninja Turtles; Charles marries Diana; Studio 54.

1990s

- **Presidents:** George H.W. Bush and Bill Clinton. The World Wide Web is born; the end of the Cold War; the Gulf War; war in Somalia, Bosnia and Yugoslavia; O.J. Simpson murder trial.

- **Music:** Seatle Grunge, Gangsta, R&B, Hip hop, Boy bands, Janet Jackson, Spice Girls, Celine Dion, Dixie Chicks, Sting, Whitney Houston, Wynona, Andrea Bocelli, the Three Tenors, Madonna and Britney Spears.

- **Film and television:**
  Films: Titanic, Dances with Wolves, Silence of the Lambs, Schindlers List, American Beauty, Forrest Gump.
  Television: Cheers, Seinfeld, Friends, Monday Night Football, E.R, Touched by an Angel, Will and Grace, Thirtysomething, The Simpsons, the View and Reality TV.

- **Dance:** Hip Hop, freestyle

- **Art:** Abstract Expressionism, graffiti.

- **Fashions:**
  Women: the return of bell bottoms, poor boy tops, the grunge look, leggings, the Goth look.
  Men: Jeans worn low on the hips, Tommy Hilfiger look, preppy looks with khaki pants and polo shirts.

- **Newsworthy:** Themed restaurants; green design products; Feng Shui; beanie babies; tickle me Elmo; video games; body piercing; Hip Hop style clothing; Tiger Woods; adventure sports; Barney; Jerry Springer; Teletubbies; cell phones; fanny packs; Y2K craze.

2000s:

- **Presidents:** George W. Bush and Barack Obama. Wars; natural disasters; the economy and the environment; the end of war in Darfur; the Sierra Leone Civil War; the September 11 attacks and the War on Terror; the Israeli-Palestinian conflict continues; the Second Congo War; war in Russia, Georgia and the Chechen Republic; The Indian Ocean earthquake; the tsunamis and Hurricane Katrina; the global financial crisis; the energy crisis; climate change; and global warming.

- **Music:** Teen pop, modern country, modern R&B and hip hop, electropop and dance, emo, alternative rock, new wave; Kelly Clarkson, Avril Lavigne, Hilary Duff, Miley Cyrus, Jonas Brothers, Britney Spears, Carrie Underwood, Taylor Swift, Beyoncé Knowles, Usher, Chris Brown, Rihanna, Eminem, 50 Cent, Lady Gaga, Cascada, Fall Out Boy, Good Charlotte, Panic At the Disco, Taking Back Sunday, Nickelback, Hinder, Coldplay, Interpol, The Killers, Kings of Leon, and Muse.

- **Film and Television:**
  Films: Gladiator, A Beautiful Mind, Chicago, Lord of the Rings Trilogy, Million Dollar Baby, Crash, the Departed, No Country for Old Men, Slumdog Millionaire, Pirates of the Caribbean trilogy, Spiderman trilogy, Harry Potter, Transformers, the Dark Knight, Avatar, The Hurt Locker.
  Television: Friends, Survivor, The OC, American Idol, Grey's Anatomy, 24, Lost, Heroes, Bones, House, Game and Reality shows.

- **Dance:** New school hip hop, break dancing, popping, street dancing.

- **Art:** Classical realism, Relational art, Street art, Stuckism, Superflat, Videogame Art, Superstroke, Virtual Art.

- **Fashions:**
  Women: Extreme low-rise distressed denim Abercrombie & Fitch look, Boho-chic and the return of skirts and dresses, colored denim, Converse "Chuck Taylor" All Stars sneakers, return of leggings, the sophisticated urban look, increasing popularity of the power suit, geek-chic designer glasses
  Men: Skinny jeans with knee-high boots.

- **Noteworthy:** The green movement; evolution of digital electronics; PDAs and smartphones; 7th Generation video games; the decline of print media; the rise of Web 2.0 and social media; adventure travel.

2010s:

- **Presidents:** _____
  _____
  _____
  _____
  _____

- **Music:** _____
  _____
  _____
  _____
  _____
  _____
  _____

- **Film and Television:** _____
  _____
  _____
  _____
  _____
  _____

- **Dance:** _____
  _____
  _____
  _____

- **Art:** _____
  _____

- **Fashion:** _____
  _____
  _____
  _____
  _____
  _____

- **Noteworthy:** _____
  _____
  _____
  _____
  _____
  _____

APPENDIX

A

Academy Awards
Adventure
An Affair of the Heart
African Safari
Aladdin
Alcatraz
Alice in Wonderland
An Alien Invasion
All That Glitters
All that Jazz
Alpine Adventure
Amazon
American Idol
Animal Kingdom
Apollo
April Fools
1001 Arabian Nights
Arctic Blast
Arthurian Tales
Atlantis
Avatar Adventure

B

Back to the Future
Ballet
Barbary Coast
Basque Revelry
Batman
Be My Valentine
Beach
Beach Boys
Beauty and the Beast
Big Band Memories
Billion Dollar Affair
Black and White Affair
Boardwalk
Books and Bards
Booty Hunt
Braveheart
Break the Dawn
The Breakfast Club
Breakfast of Champions
Broadway Baby

C

Cabaret
California Dreamin'
Candyland
Caribbean Straw Market _ Not really sure what a Straw Market is. Caribbean theme may be able to stand alone.
Carnival
Cartoon & Characters
Casablanca
Casino
Castles and Caves
Catch Me If You Can
Cavalcade of Stars
Chinese New Year's Celebration
Cinco de Mayo Fiesta
A Cinderella Story
Cirque de Cirque
Clambake
Clue
Color Themes
Comedy Festival
Comedy Night
Countries
Country Carnival
Country Fair
Country Western
Crime and Punishment
The Chocolate Affair

D

101 Dalmatians
Dancing in the Moonlight
Dancing Through Life
Dancing Through the Decades
Dancing Under the Stars
Dancing with the Stars
Daze of Our Lives
Day and Night
Day at the Ascot

Day at the Races
Denim and Diamonds
Diamonds Are a Girl's Best Friend
Disney
Doppelganger Revelry
Down Home Country Ball Dr. Seuss's Seussville
Drums of the Pacific

E

Earth Day Dreams
Election Madness
Electric Slide
Elizabethan Feast
Elvis
Enchanted Evening
English Garden Party
Entertainment Revue
Entourage
ET
Ethnic Street Party
An Evening at the Museum
An Evening in Paris
An Evening in the Park
An Evening of Magic and Illusion
Every Day's a Holiday
Exotic

F

Fairytales Come True
Family Feud
Fantasy Island
Festival of Light
Festive Festivities
Fish Story
Focus on Food
Football Kick-Off Theme
Fourth of July Celebration
Freaky Friday
Free for All
Friday Night Lights

Friday the 13th
Fright Fest
Fun in the Sun
Funky Town

G

49ers Goldrush
Dora the Explorer
Games Come to Life
Gangs of New York
GhostBuster's Party
Girl's Best Friend
Girls Just Wanna Have Fun
Gladiator
Go Diego Go
Go Green
Go West!
The Godfather
Gold Rush Days
Gold-digger
Golden Girls
Golden Jubilee
Goodfellas
Grand Prix
Great American Party
Great Gatsby
Greek Gods and Goddesses
Green is Beautiful
Green with Envy
Guitar Hero
Gypsies

H

Hall of Fame
Halloween Party
Happy Birthday - Murder Mystery
Happy Hanukkah
Happy New Year
Harry Potter
Harvest Party
Haunted House Happenings
Hawaii

Healthy Happenings
Heaven and Hell
Hillbilly Hoedown
Hip, Hip, Hooray!
Hip Hop
Hollywood Canteen Party
Homecoming Dance
Hooray for Hollywood
Hubble Sensations

I

I Am...
I Spy
Ice Age
Incredible Hulk
Indiana Jones
International Relations
Irish
Island Fever

J

Jack in the Box
James Bond – 007
Jaws
Jazz Age
Jeans, Jazz, and Jewels
Jersey Shore
Jigsaw Puzzle Competition
Journey
Jungle Fever
Jurassic Park

K

Kaleidoscopes and Prisms
King Arthur
King Kong
Kingdom of Hearts
Kings and Queens
KISS Me Gene Simmons
Kites and Other Flying Things
Knights at (of) the Roundtable

Kung Fu

L

Ladies Leading the Way
Latin/Salsa
Laughter is the Best Medicine
Legend of the Lost Leader
Locker Room
Lonely No More
Look-A-Like Cabaret
Lord of the Rings
Lunar Eclipse

M

Mad Men
Mardi Gras
Match
Maui Wowie
Medieval Feast
Men in Black
Mexican Fiesta
Midnight Madness
Monarchy Madness
Money, Money, Money
Monopoly
Monte Carlo Evening
Moon Madness
Moulin Rouge
Murder Mystery
Music Mania
Mythology

N

Never Say Never
New England Clam-bake
New Year's Eve Anytime
New Year's Eve
New York State of Mind
Newlyweds
Nickelodeon
A Night at the Museum

A Night in the Pacific
A Night in Vienna
A Night on the Orient Express
Nuts and Bolts

O

Oktoberfest
Old Country
Old Tuscan Evening
Oldies and Favorites
Olympic
On the Rocks
On Top of the World
Once Upon a Dream
Orange County
Oscar Nights
The Outback

P

Pacific Rim
Pajama Party
Panic Room
Pep Rally
Peter Pan
Phantom of the Opera
Photo Safari
Pick and Choose
Picnics
Piece of Cake
Pinocchio
Pirate Parody
Pirates of the Caribbean
Political Rally
Ponderosa Party
Poor and Homeless
Popping Bottles
Popping Champagne
Power Rangers
Press Call
Primetime
Prince and Princesses
Progressive Event (change tables, rooms, location for each course)
Prohibition Era
Puttin' on the Ritz

Q

Queen of Hearts
Queer Eye for the Straight Guy
Quest for...

R

Rags to Riches
Rainforest Café
Rally
Random Relations
Razzle Dazzle
Reach for the Stars
Red Carpet
Regatta
Reggae
Renaissance
Renew and Relax
Renew Vows
Return of the ...(Fill in the Blank)
Revenge is Sweet
Rhapsody in Pink
Rio Carnivale
Ritzy
Roaring 20's Speakeasy
Robin Hood
Rock and Roll 60's Party
Rodeo Round Up
A Roman Holiday
Russia

S

Safari
Salute to the Stars
Santa Baby
Savvy Singles
Scavenger Hunt
Serenade
Serendipity
Serenity

Sesame Street

Shipwrecks

Shogun

Silver Bullet

Silver Screen

Sin City

Single Ladies

Singles Mingles

Snow

Sock Hop

Something Old, Something New, Something Borrowed, Something Blue

South Beach

South of the Border

Southwest Sunsets

Space Odyssey

Space Frontier

Speakeasy

Spin and Twirl

Spongebob Squarepants

Sports Club

St. Patrick's Day

A Star Studded Night

Star Wars

Stars and Stripes

Sting

Streets of San Francisco

Strings, Sparkles, Champagne

Sugar and Spice

Sunday Fun Day

Sunny Days

Surfer Dude

Sweet and Sour

Sweet and Spicy

Sweets and Treats

Swing

T

Tailgate Party

Tarzan

Tastings

Tea Party

Texas Tycoon Party

Tex-Mex Fiesta

Text Mex

The Terminator

Thirsty Thursday

This is Your Life Party

Through the Looking Glass

Thunder and Lightning

Timeless

Titanic

Toga Time

Top Gun

Town and Country

Trains, Planes, and Automobiles

Transformers

Treasure Hunt

Trivial Salute

Turn the Beat Around

Tuscany Treasures

Twilight

Twister

U

Under the Stars

Under the Tuscan Sun

Underdog

Underworld

Universal

Untouchable

Up, Up and Away – All things that fly

Utopian Paradise

V

V for Victory

Valentine's Day

Vampires

Vanity Fair

Vaudeville

Versaille – Reflections in the Mirror

Vice is Nice

Victorian Party

Villa Roma

Virginia City Saloon

Viva Las Vegas

Vogue

W

Wacky Wednesday

Way Out

The Way We Were

West Side Story

Western Hoedown

Whale of an Evening

What's Your Sign?

When the Stars Align

Where's the Beef?

Whodunnit?

Wicked

Wild, Wild West

Willy Wonka's Chocolate Factory

Windows of the World

Wine and Dine

Wine Harvest

Winter Wonderland

Witches and Warlocks

Wizard of Oz

X

X-Files

X-Men

XOXO

X-Rays

Xtreme (Fill in the Blank)

X-Treme Team

X-Traordinary

Y

The Young and the Restless

Yesterday

Yin and Yang

Yoga Toga

You're the Tops

Young at Heart

Young Love

Youthfest

Youth of the Nation

Z

Zainy Brainy

Zealous

Zeus & the Olympians

Zombieland

Zoos and Zebras

Zoro

APPENDIX B: MEETING THEMES*

A

Accelerating Change

Accent on Achievement

Accent on Excellence

Accent on Action

Accent on YEAR

Acknowledging Achievements

Achieving Success

Act Now

Anything's Possible

Away We Go

Awarding Excellence

B

Back to Basics

Back to Business

Be A Winner

Be the Best

Beat the Heat

Best of the Best

Big is Beautiful

Blast Off for Success

Blueprint for Action

Breaking the Rules

Bridging the Gap

Building New Tracks

Building the Future

Building Together

Building Tomorrow

Business Builders

C

Call to Action

Campaign to Win

Capturing New Concepts

Catch the Spirit

Cause to Celebrate

Challenging Greatness

Challenge of Champions

Change Now

Change Faster

Changing for Growth

Charting New Directions

Charting Your Course

Circle of Excellence

Circle of Honor

Climbing Higher

Climbing to the Top

Count Down

Creativity Counts

Creative Solutions

Creativity Unleashed

Cutting Edge

D

Dare to be Great

Dealer's Choice

Defining Direction

Designing Directions

Determined to Win

Directing the Course

Discover New Directions

Discover Differences

Doing It Right

Driven to Greatness

Double Take

Durability Counts

E

Eager to Earn

Eager to Learn

Easy Does It

East Meets West

Eat. Drink. Work

Efficiency Rules

Eliminate Excess

Embrace Enlightenment

Encore to Greatness

Encouraging Teamwork

Endless Opportunities

Engaging the Winners

Envision the Vision

Everyone Wins Together

Exchanging Ideas

Extraordinary Ordinary Results

Eyes on the Future

F

Fabulous Facts

Face to Face

Face Meet

Facilitating Change

Fact Finding Frenzy

Failure Not an Option

Fast Tracks

Fascination

Fasten Your Seatbelts

Fearless and Famous

Finding the Answers

Flying High

Focus on Greatness

Follow Your Inspiration

Forecasting Change

Foresee the Future

Framing the Picture

Free to Grow

Free Thinking

G

Game Plan

Gaining and Growing

Gear for Growth

Gear for Success

Generating

Genius at Work

Get in Gear

Get it Together

Get Together to Grow

Getting in Gear

Go for It!

Goal Makers Mark

Going Places Together

Going for the Gold

Grace Under Fire

Grasping Greatness

Great Performers

Green is Good

H

Hall of Fame

Hardcore

Hardened for Strength

Healthy Solutions

Here Come the Winners

Hit the Mark

Horizons

Honor Roll

Honoring the Best

Honoring Leaders

Hope for Heroes

I

Igniting Outstanding Ideas

Igniting Initiatives

Illuminating Ideas

Imagining Anything

Initiating Change

In Search of Answers

In Search of Adventure

Imagine

Imagineering

Implementing New Direction

Impossible. Improbable. Achievable.

Infinite Possibilities

Inspiring Investment

Inventing Solutions

J

Jamboree

Join the Winners

Jump on Board

Justice for All

K

Keep it Going

Keep it Coming

Keep it Rolling

Kick the Competition

Knocking on Opportunity

Know Your Power
Knowledge is Power

L
Lead the Way
Leading Through It All
Learn and Lead
Let's Get Going
Let's Roll
Lean and Mean
Lifting the Load
Lighting the Way
Linking Strengths
Looking Up
Loosen Up!

M
Maintain Balance
Make the Mark
Make It Happen
Make New Tracks
Make Your Move
Maneuver the Maze
Manifest Greatness
Master the Challenge
Meet the Masters
Meeting of Minds
Mix it Up
Move with Momentum

N
Never Give Up
New Dimensions
New Directions
New Discoveries
New Horizons
Nourish Your Investment

O
On Target
On the Mark
On the Move
Opening Channels
Opportunity Awaits
Order of _____
Overcome Obstacles

P
Pacesetters
Parade of _____
Partners in Performance
Partners in Success
Perfect Your Game
Performance Counts
Pieces to Peace
Piece by Piece
Picture the Goal
Plan to Grow
Play to Win
Pledge to Play
Power of Participation
Power of People
Power of Performance
Power of Pride
Power of Products
Power of Service
Pride and Principles
Prized Possessions
Prologue to Progress
Pursue with Purpose

Q
Quest for Adventure
Question Everything
Quicken the Pace
Quota Busters

R
Race to Win
Raise the Bar
Reach for the Goal
Reach for the Stars
Ready for Change
Rewarding Perseverance
Ride with the Winners
Ride the Wave
Right the Way
Rise Above it All
Right Stuff
Road to Success
Route to Win

S
Safety First
Sale Away
Sale to Success
Salute to Success
Save the>>>>>>
Scope the Possibilities
Seize the Possibilities
Set the Pace
Shaping Your Destiny
Share the Benefits
Shoot for the Stars
Show Your Best
Soar for More
Speak Out
Spot On
Stay the Course
Strike It Big
Swing into _____

T
Take Aim
Take it Away
Taming the Team
Team Up
The Big _____
The Game is On
The Show Goes On
The Time to Win
The Tough Get Going
Time is Now
Tie it all Together
Tipping Point
Together Everyone Achieves More (TEAM)
Turn Things Around Now/Together/Faster

U
Uncommon Commonalities
Under and Over It
Understanding to Win
Unite to Strengthen
United to Win
Upward and Onward

V
Value Valor
Variety for Victory
Victory for the Team
Virtual Victory
Visible Visions
Vision Quest

W
We've Got the Power
Will to Win
Winner's Choice
Winner's Circle
Winning Combination
World of Choices
World of Difference
World of Winning

X
X-Traordinary
_____

Y
Year of Achievement
Year of Growth
Yes, We Can
Yes, You Can
You Make the Difference
You Matter to Us!

Z
Zero and Counting
Zest is Best
Zone In

*Some references from "Book of Themes" Meetings and Motivational Library©

The list of possibilities is endless ... but here's a start.

A
Airline hanger
Airport Terminal
Antique Shop
Aquarium
Arboretum
Arcade
Arena
Art Gallery
Athletic Facility
Atrium
Auditorium

B
Ballroom
Bank
Bar
Barn
Beach
Boardwalk
Boat
Bookstore
Botanical Garden
Bowling Alley
Brewery
Brownstone

C
Casino
Castle
Cathedral
Church
Circus
Club
Concert Hall
Conference Center
Country Club
Cruise Ship

D
Department Store
Desert
Dude Ranch

E
Embassy

F
Fairground
Farm

G
Gallery
Garden
Golf Club
Grand Prix

H
Health Club
Hotel

I
Ice Rink
Island Retreat

J
Jewelery Shop

K
Kitchen (in restaurant)

L
Landmark
Library
Loft

M
Mall
Mansion
Military Base
Monument
Movie Studio
Museum
Music Hall

N
Night Club

O
Oasis

P
Palace
Park
Parking Garage
Pier
Polo Club
Poolside
Private Home
Prop Gallery

R
Racetrack
Restaurant
Resort
Riding School
Rodeo
Rooftop (but set up safety barriers and make sure you are in compliance with local regulations)

S
School
Ship
Ski Resort
Specialty Store
Stadium
Street (choose it carefully, get a permit)
Studio

T
Tavern
Tea House
Temple
Tennis Court
Tent (big, of course)
Theatre (movie or stage)
Theme Park
Train

U
University

V
Veterans Hall

W
Warehouse
Winery

Y
Yacht

Z
Zoo

This section is dedicated to my friend, Tony Carey. Tony's legacy is fittingly described not as a man of few words but a man of many words.

About eight years ago, Tony and I sat in a train station somewhere in New Jersey discussing the concept of this book. Tony suggested we collaborate and that, if I were focusing on "What Color is Your Event," that he would focus on "What Scent is Your Event.' We joked about the implications of scent, and spoke of the science of using essential oils to affect temperaments, elevate moods and enhance environment. Scent, like color, is an important tool for event design.

For example, grapefruit heightens mental clarity; lavender calms and strengthens nerves; rosemary heightens mental lucidity; spearmint is uplifting. At any time, one must be prudent in using any scent professionally – and this applies to floral scents as well – due to people's allergies. Those trained in the application of pure essential oils know how potent the effects can be. One of the more popular trends over recent years has been including hookah stations at events. The tobacco that comes with this is flavored in a variety of scents, adding to the experience.

Fragrance has been treasured and respected since the beginning of time. Frankincense and myrrh have as much enduring resonance as parsley, sage, rosemary and thyme. Why? Because emotions connect so powerfully to smell. Given that our sense of smell has a strong relationship to our emotional intelligence, I can safely presume any reader of these words has a recollection of a person, place or thing that is powerfully connected to a specific scent — whether it be the smell of food, beverage, tobacco, perfume, wood, flowers, trees, plants, or any of a thousand other elements. We also have strong emotional associations to situations where a fragrance or smell was overpowering.

Add this sensory element to your palette, and you will add a different dimension to the event.

Write down a meeting message you feel best suits each enhancer. Answer suggestions are listed at bottom of the page.

Novelty Hats	Dice	Comb	Footprint
1. Message:_____	2. Message:_____	3. Message:_____	4. Message:_____

Magnifying Glass	Ruler	Piggy Bank	Light Bulb
5. Message:_____	6. Message:_____	7. Message:_____	8. Message:_____

Ace	Glasses	Binoculars	Inflatable Guitar
9. Message:_____	10. Message:_____	11. Message:_____	12. Message:_____

ANSWERS/SUGGESTIONS: 1. "Put On Your Thinking Cap", 2. "Get Ready & Roll" 3. "Go Over the Details with a Fine Tooth Comb", 4. "One Step at a Time", or use for directions to the meeting rooms; 5. "Focus on the Fine Print", or "A Clear Message"; 6. "Measure our Success", or "Growing Together"; 7. Numerous ways for budget/finance, "How Can We Save Money?" 8. Creative Session; "I See the Light!" 9. "Play Your Cards Right!" or "Your an Ace!" 10. "What Do You See?" or "Lets Lok At Some Ways To Change/Fix/Develope _____." 11. Looking to the Future; 12. Working in Concert

For an industry list by special interest groups, please refer to: Convention Industry Council www.conventionindustrycouncil.org

For global video news and up-to-the minute coverage for meetings, events, incentives, conferences, visit www.Meetings:review.com

Following is a list of some trade associations you may choose to join.

American Institute of Floral Designers
www.aifd.org

Exhibit Designers and Producers Association
www.edpa.com

Financial and Insurance Conference Planner
www.ficpnet.com

Hospitality Sales and Marketing Association International www.hsmai.org

International Advertising Association. www.iaaglobal.org

International Association of Corporate Entertainment www.iacep.com

International Association of Fairs and Exhibitions www.fairsandexpos.com

International Festival and Events Association www.ifea.com

International Interior Design Association www.iida.org

International Special Event Society www.ises.com

Meeting Professionals International www.mpiweb.org

National Association of Catering Executives www.nace.net

Professional Conference Management Association www.pcma.org

Promotional Products Association International www.ppa.org

Public Relations Society of America www.prsa.org

Women In Communications www.wici.org

PUBLICATIONS AND TRADE MAGAZINES

Association Now - www.asaecenter.org

Best Events - www.besteventsmag.com

BizBash – www.bizbash.com

Business Travel News – www.btnonline.com

Convene – www.pcma.org/Convene.htm

Corporate and Incentive Travel www.themeetingmagazines.com

Corporate EVENT Magazine www.exhibitoronline.com/corpevent

Corporate Meetings & Incentives – www.meetingsnet.com/corporatemeetingsincentives

Event Design www.eventdesignmag.com

Event Marketer - www.eventmarketer.com

Event Solutions – www.event-solutions.com

EXPO Magazine – www.expoweb.com/magazines

Hotel F&B Executive – www.hotelfandb.com

IAAM - www.iaam.org/Facility_manager/Pages/Facility_Issues.htm

Masterplanner – www.masterplanneronline.com

Medical Meetings – www.meetingsnet.com/medicalmeetings

MeetingNews – www.mimegasite.com

M&C – www.meetings-conventions.com

One+ - www.mpiweb.org/Magazine

Religious Conference Manager – www.meetingsnet.com/religiousconferencemanager

Smart Meetings – www.smartmeetings.com/issues

Special Events Magazine – www.specialevents.com

SportsTravel Magazine – www.sportstravelmagazine.com

Successful Meetings – www.mimegasite.com

Tradeshow Week – www.tradeshowweek.com

I was scheduled to teach a class in event management at New York University in September of 2001. The first class was to take place on September 18th. As we all remember, New York City was attacked one week earlier.

Despite the catastrophic events that had occurred, I knew the one vital thing that virtually all New Yorkers now accepted was the importance of coming together. I also knew I had to put the situation in perspective for my own class and acknowledge that their attendance was the start of their own (and my) personal healing.

I contacted two former students, both named Lisa and both of whom had been working as event planners for a major hotel at the World Trade Center on the day of the attack. I encouraged them to speak to the class about what they had gone through, and they agreed. All 30 students showed up for class and listened as these young ladies recounted and shared their story of 9/11.

They told us that there had been a huge tremor in the hotel. Working with hotel security, they immediately evacuated five breakfast meetings which were being held simultaneously in the hotel. Their general manager then asked them to work together do a sweep of the entire hotel, from the top floor down, in order to evacuate the building. While they were in the process of doing this, they came across a television tuned to CNN, and realized that the nearby Twin Towers had been attacked, which explained the building tremors and the vibration. They kept calm, completed the sweep of the hotel, and got all the guests out of the building. They themselves were two of the last five people out of the hotel.

When the first tower collapsed, these two women took cover in open elevator shaft and hid in horror as debris rained down all around them. They waited until the roaring sound of buildings collapsing around them subsided, then began to climb over mountains of rubble, hoping to make their way to safety and find a way home.